GW01458710

This book is a must-read if...

◊ you need a guide to find your own purpose;

◊ you want to immerse yourself in a journey of discovery;

◊ you want to make a difference to your community and the world around you;

◊ you need motivation to galvanise you into action;

◊ you are searching for your self-belief;

◊ you want to uncover the secrets of positive thinking, passion and determination;

◊ you want to learn how to move forward with your life;

◊ you want inspiration from a community champion;

◊ you are interested in family history and memoirs;

◊ you want to explore the history of Nigerian experience in the UK.

Words of Love

"I met Kate Anolue whilst working as a Consultant Obstetrician and Gynaecologist at the North Middlesex University Hospital NHS Trust in Enfield. Kate was a Senior Midwife at the hospital and I was greatly impressed with her energy, sense of service to the community, and constant desire to help others. This hard-working, single mother of four children then undertook a law degree whilst continuing to work night shifts, all in a bid to develop and equip herself to help others. As the Royal College of Midwife's (RCM) Steward at our hospital, she was always tenaciously defending and supporting any midwives that were involved in cases of medical negligence.

Kate is a woman who exudes warmth, professionalism and drive, and is someone who never puts herself first. This is demonstrated by her many accomplishments, including her tenures as the Mayor of the London Borough of Enfield not once, but twice! Her latest book, *Time for Purpose*, reflects all these strengths and more.

It has been interesting to learn about Kate's childhood and teenage years in Nigeria and to see how these shaped the course of her life on emigrating to the UK. It is wonderful to see Kate bring her enthusiasm, verve and purpose to life in *Time for Purpose* and I thoroughly recommend the book as a masterpiece."

Professor Stanley Okolo
Director General of West Africa Health Organisation
Diplomat, Leader and Executive Coach
Former Professor and Consultant Gynaecologist,
North Middlesex University Hospital NHS Trust

"*Time for Purpose* is a thorough study of purpose narrated through the lens and pen of Dr Kate Anolue, as she takes us through pertinent moments of her life. All her experiences point towards her purpose and she invites us to undertake the same life review. I would recommend this book to everyone who has ever sought their purpose or wanted confirmation that they are on the right path to their purpose."

Ihuaku Patricia Nweke, BSc, MSc, MCIPS
Founder and CEO of Cedarcube
Founder and Chair of International Consortium for Domestic Peace
Director of I.Kollection fashion

"Having a book in hand is normally not my thing. I am a thinker with little expression, even though I set up the first black and ethnic television in Europe, BEN Television. But having *Time for Purpose* in my inbox for review and comment pushed my interest to read more when I clicked Chapter One: Purpose.

There is no doubt that Cllr Kate Anolue spent considerable time to research and bring to life her own experience, family background, cultural difference – needed more than ever today – and educational pursuits in this book. On top of all that, she demonstrates her undeniable passion for tirelessly helping others in every aspect of her life.

Time for Purpose is split into 10, easy to read chapters, packed with Cllr Kate's wisdom and philosophies. There truly is something for everyone in this book.

Crowning the experience and perspective of life from Cllr Kate (widely known as Aunty Kate!), *Time for Purpose* shows us an invaluable and measured criteria to succeed in life."

Mentoring Cmdt Alistair Soyode
Founder of BEN Television,
Former Chairman of Nigerian in Diaspora Organisation (NIDO/E),
Commandant, International Mentoring Corp.

"This is a must-read for anyone looking for the drive they need to pursue their goals in the face of adversity.

Kate Anolue is an incredible woman whose determination and force of spirit is an inspiration to me and all those who know and work with her.

Time for Purpose tells Kate's story of someone who has never stopped championing diversity, and working to make communities stronger."

The Honourable Feryal Clark
MP for Enfield North

"Dr Kate Anolue's new book *Time for Purpose* is an inspiring read which will galvanise you into action. Her enthusiasm, relentless determination and drive are all on display in the very accessible book. Having worked for several years with Kate as a councillor for Enfield before I won my parliamentary seat, as well as campaigning together for all the elections in the Borough, I know first-hand what a powerhouse of energy and resilience she is. We have attended numerous fundraising events together and I can testify that Kate is an absolute role model for many with her championing of diversity and strength of community spirit."

The Honourable Bambos Charalambous
MP for Enfield Southgate

"A thought-provoking collection of life lessons, shared earnestly, in a very relatable manner. The book advises its audience to believe in themselves and the power of a positive mindset while pursuing purpose, but it also cautions against expecting overnight success or an easy road. The book is applicable to readers' real lives and situations, balanced by anecdotes from Dr Kate Anolue. *Time for Purpose* is a great mirror that prompts one to reflect on one's life."

Dr Peter Ozua, MBBS, FRCPath
Consultant Histopathologist, Basildon University Hospital, UK

"What a riveting, thrilling, soul searching, inspiring, rich and reassuring piece of thought.

The hero which some people aspire to be is within them, but not being purposeful enough, a lot of time is wasted chasing others' dreams and the heroes in them instead.

The message in Kate Anolue's *Time for Purpose* is:

Be purposeful, look inward, and find the hero in you through focusing on yourself instead of what cultures, traditions, social, or societal norms constantly dictate.

Be purposeful. Be focused. Be confident. Be bold to be different. Self-affirm.

Be you, and unleash your genius."

Jenny Chika Okafor
Lawyer, Civil Rights Advocate, Empowerment Coach
Founder, Nigerian Women In Diaspora Leadership Forum (NWIDLF)

"*Time for Purpose* is a wonderful book where you can focus on your purpose as who you were created to be. You come to the realisation that you were created for purpose, which is life-changing. Once you realise your purpose, you will be more passionate and able to fulfil your dreams. Aunty Kate walks you through her life – the highs and the lows – and how she managed to find her purpose and life authentically. Through her own story, she prompts you to think about your own life and purpose as she ends each chapter with "Aunty Kate's Learning Points".

I highly recommend this book."

Dayo Olomu
Amazon Bestselling author of 'The Premium Leader: Leadership Attributes and Strategies for Today's Volatile World'

"Councillor Kate Anolue grew up in a typical African environment where circumstances thrust her into a position of leadership without it actually being planned. One of the tragedies of Africa, is that as a continent, she has not invested in leadership and sought to fish out individuals like Councillor Anolue and groom them for leadership roles.

Just to give you an example of this 'accidental' leadership, as the first female child of her parents, or the "Ada" of the family as it is known in Igboland, Cllr Anolue had to assume a minor mothering role. She grew up with her parents and six siblings and being the firstborn was catapulted automatically into a position of responsibility.

As *Time for Purpose* highlights, at certain points during her adolescence, Cllr Anolue felt that on many occasions when she was looking after her younger brothers and sister, she was like a mum to them. As is always the case in an African setting, elder girls do not actually mind it, as they thrive on the responsibility.

Generally, girls who excel in such environments, tend to go on to continue with leadership roles at school, as was the case with Kate. At school, she found herself being given positions of responsibility such as vice prefect and rather than recoil, she actually started to ask, why not actual prefect?!

Time for Purpose exposes the lack of African leadership development programmes as a girl who has shown leadership roles in her family at a tender age and then later at school with prefectural roles, should be a prime candidate for national leadership positions. Leadership at home or school should constitute preparation for more significant experiences in life's journey."

Ayo Akinfe
Chairman, Central Association of Nigerians in the UK
Author of two books about Nigeria, 'Fuelling the Delta Fires' and 'Black Ladder'
Columnist for several publishing houses in Nigeria and the UK
Founding Editor of Nigerian Watch, UK-based paper for the UK's Nigerian community

"Right from the start as a 15-year-old, Kate Anolue knew exactly what she wanted out of life. And the remarkable thing is that she saw all her earmarked goals in her mental imageries. What an empirical and experiential story in this book!

Time for Purpose acts as an inspiration to those of us that are demoralised one way or another as single parents; as well as those witnessing one challenge or another in their marital and family lives.

Indeed, it is my candid advice that Dr Kate Anolue should be adopted/ nominated as a role model and mentor to young and adults alike; and should be appointed a senior fellow in any UK and Nigerian universities, so to teach our young and elderly ones what can be done to save their respective lives and families, because she has the cognate experiences that lied dormant in her brain, awaiting to be tapped for the benefit of humankind to achieve their own goals.

Most importantly, this book is not meant for women alone, as the act that its application is universal in nature – and can be applied in globally in any country.

Finally, the remarkable thing that Kate explains, is that no matter the predicament one must have witnessed in life, adversity is part of life. We can use it as a learning curve that enables us to achieve our own goals in life – provided we know our mission of what we want out of life. *Time for Purpose* is a wonderful case study for us to all to learn from."

Professor Poly Ike Emenike, MON.
Author of 10 books
Member of the Board and Senior Lecturer at
University of Zik Business School (UBS), Awka and Lagos, Nigeria.

This book is dedicated to my siblings, children,
my three granddaughters and two grandsons,
both born during coronavirus lockdown in 2020.
You all bring joy to my life. Thank you.

To all widows, single mothers and girl child.
I hope my experiences in this book help you to find purpose.

To all my long-time friends who have passed away,
you were part of my journey and have always been there for me:
Blossom Davidson, Carmel Steele
and HRH Helen Ogbu (Anuka).
May your souls rest in perfect peace. AMEN.

Feeling lost? Wanting more? Looking for direction?

TIME FOR PURPOSE

How one indomitable woman's experiences fuelled
her discipline, determination and dedication
to drive her passion for serving others.

Dr Kate Anolue

First published in Great Britain in 2022
by Book Brilliance Publishing
265A Fir Tree Road, Epsom, Surrey, KT17 3LF
+44 (0)20 8641 5090
www.bookbrilliancepublishing.com
admin@bookbrilliancepublishing.com

A CIP catalogue record for this book is available
at the British Library.

ISBN 978-1-913770-49-5.

Typeset in Calibri.
Printed by 4edge Ltd.

Contents

Foreword

H.E. Dr. O. Favour Ayodele

As an African man, it is wonderful to see an African sister excel in the field of her choice.

Dr Kate Anolue is the epitome of a person who sets a goal, focuses on the action she needs to take, then fuelled with her determination, tenacity and resilience, ensures she achieves whatever she sets her mind to achieve.

From an early age, it is easy to see in her book *Time for Purpose* that, despite having to care for her six younger siblings, study at school and survive a civil war, she made no excuses to chase her dream. As an African woman, there is a perceived outcome for what she may achieve; however, it is thanks to her father, a man of a different vision, who gave his daughter the direction, space and encouragement she needed to pursue a shared dream.

As a woman of courage, Dr Kate Anolue left her beloved African home in Nanka, Anambra State, Nigeria, to join her spouse and seek a better life in England, UK. Here she settled down with her husband and made a home and career for herself as a midwife. Despite having four children to look after, she made no excuses but kept on going to provide for her family, always finding solutions to the challenges she faced. One of the biggest challenges was when she found herself widowed and left with four young children to raise by herself, the youngest being only 18 months old.

Again, her resilience was exemplary as she knew, regardless of her pain, she was now the breadwinner and had to continue working to provide for her children. In *Time for Purpose*, she talks about how when faced with trauma and pain, finding something else that needs your full attention can be a saving grace and help you through the tough times.

Education has always featured prominently in the life of Dr Kate, and she once again followed her heart and dream by completing a law degree at the age of 48. She knew that by graduating in law, she could do more as a midwife; she would be able to advise many mothers and the midwives at first hand when it came to matters of medical negligence.

Always looking to serve the public more, Dr Kate continued working in her community. After retiring from her midwifery post, she worked tirelessly for the betterment of her people and was able to put all of her focus and energy into the political arena. Not content with being the Mayor of the Borough of Enfield once, she managed to be elected for a second time, a brilliant accomplishment for a black African woman. As a champion of young people, she instigated the position of a young Mayor in her Borough. This innovative concept is now streamed into the council's Annual General Meeting at the Mayor-making process.

Her work continues to be recognised and she was honoured with the Freedom of the Borough of Enfield in 2007. Her work is not only acknowledged here in the UK, but also in Nigeria where she is Chieftain in her home town of Nanka. Her title name is Adajere Mba Tulugo – meaning 'Our daughter that went to a foreign land and brought us Glory'.

She continues to work constantly for her community in Enfield as a local councillor and was re-elected in May 2022, establishing her as a long-serving councillor with over 20 years' service.

In *Time for Purpose*, Dr Kate shares her values, philosophy and wisdom for the next generation of women, inspiring and empowering them to go after their dreams, knowing they can achieve anything they want to be in life, and to "never say never!"

'No HOPE is hopeless in itself'.

Dr. Favour Ayodele is a life coach; author; education, business & management consultant; certified counsellor; philanthropist; humanitarian; and international keynote speaker. He is the Vice President of West-Africa of The World Economic Forum for Asia-Africa WEFAA. He is also a Nigerian Presidential Aspirant for 2023.

He has 20 years of groundbreaking experience in administration, business/corporate management and is a dynamic multinational award-winning leadership expert who has been in the business of capacity building for two decades. He is a self-taught multiskilled strategist and was a professional footballer who enjoys what he does.

He has hosted scholars in intentional pragmatic approaches on political-economic integration, gender-based violence, racialism, governance, democracy, climate change, youth and women in leadership, food security, children education, social-cultural and gender parity, environment, and mind rehabilitation. He has engaged distinguished leaders on national and global community projects.

Introduction

"Midwifery is my profession
but inspiring women is my mission!"

All of my working life has been devoted to supporting women, from bringing new life into the world, to elevating them to a place where they believe in themselves and create the life of their dreams.

Having lived more than seventy years, it is about time I share my experience, expertise and wisdom with a new generation of women. It is my duty to leave an imprint on this world as part of my legacy, along with the difference I have made in the world as a single mother, midwife, community champion and leader. I have learned the difference between influencing and making a lasting impact by my interactions because of the way in which I leave people feeling. How do I know? They tell me!

Inspiration for *Time for Purpose* came after I had written and self-published my memoir, *Kate Anolue, Autobiography*. Yes, it told my story, but what was lacking was the impact of my life. Sharing how to create your destiny by taking control of your mindset, your path and discovering your purpose which gives meaning to your life.

Many of the traumas, experiences and events in my life are shared by millions of women around the world. As a Nigerian woman in diaspora, like many of my sisters, I am a very ambitious woman who is driven to succeed and make a difference in the world. By writing this book, I know that it will help and guide many women on their journey to realising themselves, their purpose and mission.

My experiences of being a midwife, community champion and single mother showed me that many women who find themselves alone in bringing up children think that their lives are over. They believe they have no future and if they are a woman of colour, this is intensified because they do not have a sense of belonging. With this closed mindset, they do not push themselves and prefer to do menial jobs rather than allow themselves to be visible as a powerful woman.

I am driven and determined to show them that this is a lie and that they can be anything they choose when they put their mind to it. They must also find someone who will encourage and champion their efforts to transform their lives. You should neither do things alone as it will set you up for failure, nor should you tolerate anyone who disrespects and discourages you and your potential. Once you find like-minded people, you can tap into their experiences, and through collaboration, achieve beyond your expectations.

Each chapter is filled with stories; not just my own, but the universal evidence that we all seek to support transforming limiting beliefs to a new belief that we can adopt as truth. The human mind loves stories and I have also included some metaphors that aid understanding of human traits, such as feeding a negative or positive mindset with your thoughts. This is illustrated in the metaphor about the two wolves.

Also within each chapter is the philosophy I have developed over my lifetime based on my experience, expertise and education. Teaching the learnings of life is rooted in the insight and growing wisdom that age brings, and the voice of our elders is one that has to be listened to wholly, with a respect for accomplishments and actions that reflects my Nigerian culture. I am an Igbo woman from the east, one of the three main tribes in Nigeria, where education is paramount in the lives of its people because it provides a better future, relieves you from poverty, and offers many opportunities in life. The wisdom reveals the legacy that I wish to leave behind.

Within each chapter, you will be inspired by quotes and Aunty Kate's Learning Points. These are the 'how-tos' of transforming your life. The only way you can create change is through action. Thoughts and words alone are not enough. As the cliché states, "actions speak louder than words." My life demonstrates that through integrity, you must walk your talk to be the role model for those who come behind you. People are always looking to be inspired into action, but it takes more than action to sustain and fuel activity.

The essence of *Time for Purpose* is to illustrate the human traits necessary to succeed and find happiness and fulfilment. Traits such as a positive mindset, tenacity, resilience, determination, discipline, self-belief, proactivity, adopting responsibility for your actions, and inactions. These can be honed into a powerful set of values, principles and skills that give direction to your inner compass which is based on the awareness of and knowing your values, vision and mission. Most importantly, I have lived my life with one thing that has driven me to this point – Never give up! No excuses allowed! Never say never!

Lastly, the title of this book, *Time for Purpose*, envelops the notion that there is no time like the present. The past is behind us and the future is never guaranteed. I urge you to go on the most powerful journey of your life which asks you to find the courage to enter into your inner world, face who you are, embracing the good and bad, and listen to your intuitive voice, for it knows your purpose. When you accept this as your destiny, you will begin to find meaning to your life and acknowledge that it is now ***Time for Purpose***!

Dr Kate Anolue

Chapter One: Purpose

Inner Journey, Belief, Passion

"Find a purpose in life so big it will challenge every capacity to be at your best."

David O. McKay
American educator and religious leader

Many people have written books on 'Purpose', but what does it mean? According to the Cambridge English Dictionary, purpose is defined as:

an intention or aim; a reason for doing something or for allowing something to happen

When reflecting on the meaning, I can say it confirms my understanding of what it is to live a life on purpose. I have always found myself having a solid reason for doing something. I set out each day with an intention to achieve a small goal, and when I focus on the outcome of that intention, it gives me purpose to allow it to happen.

Many people spend a lifetime trying to find their purpose, and they often give up because they are not connecting with anything of significance. People often look outside themselves to find their purpose, as their environment, culture and upbringing shape them. Their mindsets are then filled with limiting beliefs because of relationships, friendships and following traditions. You often hear statements such as, "It runs in the family." This type of statement immediately shuts down possibilities, and consequently, you do not even try to create change but accept it as a truth.

One thing to ponder is that change is part of everything. Our cells change, time moves on, and we change from generation to generation. Once you understand that change happens all of the time, it is easier to stop looking outside of yourself and turn your attention to what is happening inside you. This change in perspective is a massive paradigm shift and may take some time to register before you begin to take steps to change your thoughts, words and actions.

Humans like routine, which can create 'bad' habits, inducing people to stay inside of their comfort zones. When you adopt this habit, you can often find yourself drifting from one thing to another without purpose. The acceptance of such behaviours prevents you from questioning them. "Why am I doing this every day?", whatever 'this' is for you. Ask yourself is it out of habit or is it to attain something extraordinary, such as happiness or a goal, such as becoming a vet? A lack of purpose creates misery.

Time to think about whether or not you live with purpose or if you are drifting aimlessly from one thing to another. We are going on a journey together to find out the answers. It is time to go back to your childhood. Are you ready?

Let me tell you a story...

I grew up with my parents and six siblings in Nigeria; I was the eldest. Being the firstborn catapulted me into a position of responsibility; you could say I was born to lead. It certainly felt like that on many occasions when I would look after my younger brothers and sister, and it often felt like I was Mum to my siblings. The funny thing about that situation was that I didn't mind; I thrived on responsibility and enjoyed every moment.

School was no different for me. I soon found myself being given positions of responsibility such as vice-prefect. However, I often

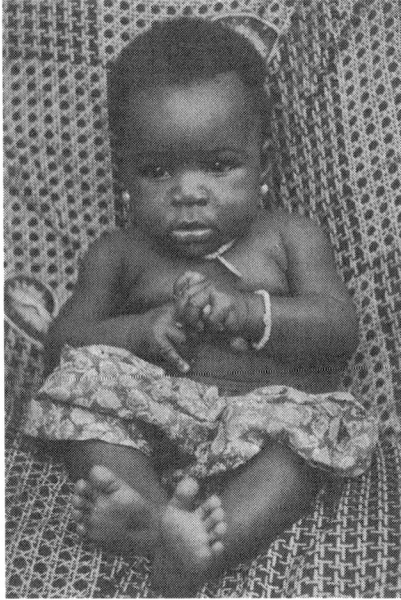

Kate as a baby

wondered why I was not the head prefect? My desire to lead was so great that I questioned everything. Eventually, I learnt what it takes to become a prefect. My commitment to being a great big sister reflected my actions at school; therefore, everyone knew me as trustworthy, which earned me more opportunities to prove I was worthy of such accolades. I liked the feelings around these positions, so it made me determined to keep on achieving my main goals.

Whether at home or school, preparation for more significant experiences would be part of my life's journey. As a child, I could not see this, but I remember focusing on the feelings I felt every time I did something worthwhile and to the best of my ability. The final story I want to share is that besides home and school, serving others was achieved every time I helped my mother at the market stall. I loved it, and people came to know me as a beneficial and loyal child who worked with her mother. I also saw myself as a grown-up, and this made me feel that I was in the right place at the right time. Hindsight is a beautiful gift, as I realised that my experiences were the nurturing ground for my life of service. I was born a Leader.

It's your turn...

Think back to your childhood. What did you love to do as a child? Is there anything you felt connected to or is reflected in your life today? Or perhaps there is something that you have left behind because of your upbringing, circumstances and experiences? You may want to stop here for a moment and write down your answers. You will be amazed at what you discover.

Early childhood experiences often signpost what lies ahead in life. The development of leadership certainly was part of my destiny. What is yours?

We can often find more evidence on purpose when we look at the lives of famous people who have been or are in the limelight. Take the great Martin Luther King. How did his childhood shape him for the future?

Martin Luther King Jr. grew up in a happy home with his father Reverend Martin Luther King Sr. and his mother, Alberta Williams King, who was also a reverend. He grew up with an older sister, Willie Christine King, and a younger brother, Alfred Daniel Williams King. His mother taught him to play the piano, and his spiritual teachings were given to him by his father and grandfather.

On a family outing to a shoe store, Martin Luther King first experienced racial inequality. His family was ushered out the back exit after the store owner told them that blacks were not allowed in the store. This incident and the growing knowledge that blacks were not allowed in restaurants, not allowed to drink from the same water fountains as white people and endured degrading injustices at the hands of white people in the south, ignited his purpose to fight for justice and change. The experiences of these early childhood days led Martin Luther King Jr. to his dynamic movement for equality.

When considering their purpose, people often ask the profound question "WHY?" Just like purpose, there are many books about finding your Why. *Start with Why* by Simon Sinek is a good introduction as it focuses on asking five whys to get to the route of the answer.

The word 'why' suggests giving a reason as your response. So to find your purpose, you need to ask questions such as, "Why is it important to find my purpose? Why am I here? Why am I doing what I do?" If you cannot find the answer, then search inside for it. If you do not like the answer, the only solution is to change it. Curiosity and adventure is the inner journey that reveals so much wisdom.

Change takes courage. Difficulty finding and choosing courage is why so many people struggle to find their purpose. They need to find the courage to change, which may take time and change their mindset, actions and habits. Change may mean you have to leave some people behind who are determined to remind you of who they think you are. It is not your thoughts but other people's thoughts, judgements and accusations that keep you in that small-minded place which imprisons you. If you want to succeed, you have to change, no matter how challenging. Have courage!

Talking of change reminds me of another story when I lived through a civil war in Nigeria which lasted from 6th July 1967 to 12th January 1970, with the official surrender papers being signed on 15th January 1970. The war experiences were a significant time in my life that have left lasting memories.

It is here that I made substantial choices, and I had to step up even more to the challenge during this period. Instead of being a big sister, I felt the need to be another mum so that I could support my parents with feeding and taking care of the younger children. It was a time to step into my leadership shoes again; perhaps I never took them off. I became proactive; I knew I could trade because of the support I gave to my mother at the market each day after school, so I used that experience to develop my confidence in trading. When you are open-minded, the opportunities you receive may be signs of your purpose. My purpose determined that I adopt a parental role as I was the eldest sibling of my family. All around me were displaced families which caused immense pain and suffering but none more so than the knowledge that children were being trafficked and abused.

This intense situation revealed yet another opportunity to commit to each day with purpose, and I had a reason to do the things I did.

Much evidence around you exemplifies life-changing events revealing purpose. None more so than the great Austrian psychiatrist and neurologist, Viktor Frankl, author of *Man's Search for Meaning*, who was imprisoned in several concentration camps, including Auschwitz. He suffered the loss of his wife and family at the hands of the Nazis. Frankl spent most of his life exploring the human struggle for survival to give others hope that not all is lost until your last breath. His message is to find greater meaning and purpose in your life.

Your turn…

Can you think of a significant time in your life that revealed your purpose? Perhaps you are still seeking meaning? I ask you to stop looking outside of you and turn your attention to your inner world. Consider your experiences because in them will lie your answer. When you live with purpose, you have grit and determination to achieve whatever it is that is your driving force – purpose.

You have no doubt heard phrases such as the ripple effect, the domino effect, and "one thing leads to another". These idioms are all true. Opposites are part of life: up, down; in, out; win, lose. You are going to focus on winning. With purpose, it makes winning much more effortless. Let us explore one more story about winning. You see, when one door closes, another one appears. Now that could be the consequence of a thought, a conversation or meeting someone. I am sure you can think of a time when you had an idea that spurred you into action, a conversation that led to a solution, and a chance meeting that enabled you to do something you may not have otherwise had the opportunity to do.

Firstly, consider that you need to change your job. That thought will spur you on to look for another job. Next, you have a conversation with a friend who shares that they heard about a role they think is made for you. Then you further explore that opportunity and consider if it is a right for you. Lastly, you meet someone in a coffee shop who tells you their workplace is hiring new staff and it is your dream job. You take immediate action and walk through that door of opportunity.

Life is like this all of the time if you have an open mind to it.

Growing up, I loved learning at school, at home and in my community. My mum took me everywhere with her from a very early age, to church and town meetings. It is no surprise then that the ripple effect of the feelings of belonging I experienced every time I learned something new that supported my purpose, whatever it was, led me to enter teacher training. I was a born leader, but I am also a born teacher.

I happily went off to teacher training college and began my next phase in life. Excitement flooded my body as I was finally making a dream come true. For years, becoming a teacher was the focus that drove me to be the best student. But let me introduce you to the 'curve ball', when something unexpectedly blocks your plans. Amid my enthusiasm, a war (which was outside of my control) blocked my path. I had no alternative but to adopt a mind that embraced change, even when I did not like its interruption, forcing me to create and carve a new path in life. However, that is part of life, so one must learn to accept change. When you go with the flow, it reduces anxiety. When you connect within, you begin to understand the power of acceptance. I learned this positive and purposeful life skill fast.

In the 1960s, arranged marriages were a part of my culture and tradition. During this time, I met my husband; the only issue was that he lived in the United Kingdom, and I was living in Nigeria! Like an obedient child, I upheld my father's wishes and moved to England, where I would meet and marry my husband. All of this happened in my final year of teacher training. I sacrificed my desire for tradition. That is a point inviting further exploration, but let me continue with my story. I am sure you have heard the saying, "Everything happens for a reason," and the reason reveals itself in hindsight. Here, I want to reiterate that acceptance is part of the master plan in determining your purpose and living it.

A starting point...

As a human, you are naturally curious. Think of the four-year-old who continually asks, "But why?" No matter your answer, it is always followed up with another "Why?" This innate trait continues throughout your life; it is powerful to start with 'why'. Keep asking questions about who you are, why you are here, and what is your purpose.

Let me take you to a place that is often dark, yet within it, at the core, is love. Our lives and cultures often create a romantic version of love. You learn to love your parents as a child, then your siblings and other friends and family. You are constantly bombarded with the media to worship celebrities, things and experiences. I want to share that the real power within you begins when you learn to love yourself. Now that is a scary thought because you often hear to think of others; you put them before yourself, and as a mother or father, you tend to put your children's needs first as their protector.

Imagine flipping this belief. You may have heard the human body referred to as a vessel. If your vessel is empty of love, how can you give love to others from its emptiness? You can't! That is why it is vital to learn how to love yourself. Short and sweet, you can fill up your 'love cup' by taking time for you to do what you love to do, whatever that may be, something that gives you that warm fuzzy feeling inside. It is easier to show more when you have replenished all the giving you do. You become less resentful and bitter. It's essential to accept yourself – the good and the bad – and love yourself.

Another way to help you love yourself more is to know your values. Your values are the driving force for everything you do. Knowing your values enables you to make decisions and take risks, and is your moral compass for everything you do. Consider when you make a 'bad' choice. A torrent of uncertainty floods your mind, and you feel that it may have been the wrong decision. When you know your values and love yourself, you can begin to create boundaries to protect yourself from outside influences. The more you practice this way of living, the clearer your purpose becomes. The truth is you know your purpose; it is that everything else gets in the way.

It is time to find more courage so let me take you deeper into yourself. You may be feeling a little lost; that's okay. Remember everything changes, and courage is the first step in providing you with a chance to change.

Let's take a trip down memory lane. Consider what you love to do. What lights you up? You may even go back into your childhood. Finding what brings you joy is key to unfolding your purpose. Acknowledge that voice within and listen to it. It reveals wisdom. Initially, you may not believe it, but accepting it will drown out all the negative chatter inside your head. It's time to silence it, listen to your heart's desire, and follow it. Recognise what is calling you and then fulfil it. That is your purpose, drive, and reason for your being.

Another powerful tool is to learn how to reflect without judgement. Look at the positives of what you have done and attach less focus on the negatives. However, failures are the best learning experiences. Take Thomas Edison, who invented the light bulb. Some intellectuals and academics argued that he took 1,000 to 10,000 attempts to create the first light bulb. The significance is that he never gave up; instead, he kept going. He did not let failure stop him from achieving his vision. The same for a child learning to ride a bicycle; they fall off and get back up again. Edison's resilience, tenacity and perseverance are precious life lessons to us all.

It is also essential that you learn to open your mind. Living with a fixed, closed mindset will shut doors of opportunity in your face. Look for the opportunity; question everything. Do not simply accept it as truth. It is your responsibility to find and live by your truth. Remember the curious child? Be that child; she/he continues to live within you. Nurture them and allow them to guide you.

Your turn...

Allow me to introduce you to your *gifts*. We all have them; the secret is knowing them. Think about a significant challenge in your life. As you reflect on it and work through each aspect, ask yourself, "What have I learned?" This questioning is a skill, a realisation, but the power lies in recognising a characteristic that is part of who you are, such as being a determined, kind person and having a good sense of humour. What have these experiences led you to do? Is what you are doing close to living with a purpose, or are you still unsure? If so, working through some of the steps in this chapter will enable you to take action and be closer to understanding why it is essential to living your life with purpose.

Find your mission in life and let it be your guiding star. Drive with your why every day, not just sometimes. Learn to love yourself more and give freely without judgement. You can create your own path, so there is no room for excuses, whining and giving up – look for the evidence within and from others who have done what you want to do.

Here is a crucial factor to living with purpose, achieving and making a difference. Do not be afraid to work hard. It takes time – it is not a quick fix, but you grow stronger every time you try. Unfortunately, many people today live with a 'microwave' mentality; they want everything quickly, now! Life is not like that in reality. It's tenacity, keeping moving and getting back up when you fall that makes the difference to you, your life and your happiness.

"My mission in life is not merely to survive,
but to thrive; and to do so with some passion,
some compassion, some humour, and some style."
Maya Angelou,
American poet, memoirist and civil rights activist

Aunty Kate's Learning Points

◊   Have a WHY.

◊   Set a goal linked to education and what you want to do with the results.

◊   Focus on what you want to achieve.

◊   Find and use evidence from your story and other peoples' stories, including metaphors.

◊ Explore and discuss obstacles and how you overcame them – connect with drive and determination and fuel it by finding your WHY.

◊ Adopt a 'No Excuses' attitude.

◊ Enjoy the process – celebrate the small wins along the way – they all add up, they compound.

One last thing...

To establish your purpose, you need to find your life's mission through something that ignites your passion. Your childhood can often reveal that passion when you discover what brought you joy as a child. It comes from the soul of your being when you still yourself and listen to your inner voice. Setting goals is a necessity; be determined and never give up even when the going gets tough. You have everything you need to be successful, feel fulfilled, and be happy; it's about learning to trust yourself, knowing that you have a higher purpose. God has given you gifts to use in this life to benefit you, others and the world.

Chapter Two: Mindset

Positivity, Open-Minded, Flexibility of Thought

"Once your mindset changes, everything on the outside will change along with it."

Steve Maraboli
American author and speaker

A positive mindset

"Every cloud has a silver lining. Always look on the bright side of life. Carry the sunny weather within you." These are just some of the everyday sayings you will know. These idioms reflect a positive mindset, a way of looking at things, people, and the world. Do your thoughts turn to negativity saying, "I can't do that; it never works out for me; no one in my family has ever…" May I suggest that these phrases are excuses? Yes, excuses. These notions or beliefs keep you stuck in a safe space. You do not even attempt to go outside your comfort zone, let alone take risks. Don't just take my word for it; Carol Dweck, author of *Mindset: The New Psychology of Success* (2006), conducted a study on mindset using her students to gather the evidence.

Dweck was puzzled that some students seemed to bounce back when they made mistakes, while others became distraught when they failed. She wanted to study students' attitudes to understand why these students responded differently. She coined the terms Fixed Mindset and Growth Mindset resulting from her study.

FIXED MINDSET	GROWTH MINDSET
Intelligence is static: This perception leads to a desire to look smart and therefore tends to: ✓ Avoid challenges ✓ Give up quickly due to obstacles ✓ See effort as no point ✓ See feedback as criticism and not useful ✓ Be threatened by others' success	Intelligence can be developed: Leads to a desire to learn and tends to: ✓ Embrace challenges ✓ Persist despite obstacles ✓ See effort as a pathway to achievement ✓ Learn from criticism and feedback ✓ Be inspired by others' success

In a TED talk, Carol Dweck claimed that "a growth mindset is when students understand that their abilities can be developed." Students who believe the mind is supple (growth mindset) can quickly bounce back from failure because they see it as a learning opportunity.

> "If parents want to give their children a gift, the best thing they can do is to teach their children to love challenges, be intrigued by mistakes, enjoy effort, and keep on learning. Their children don't have to be slaves of praise, and they will have a lifelong way to build and repair their confidence."

> Carol Dweck

Many scientists once thought that the brain's ability to change and grow happened during early childhood. Since then, neuroscience research indicates that the brain is much more malleable and continues to change into old age.

"The brain is constantly creating and destroying neural pathways, forming the thought and behaviour patterns our brain uses to make decisions, choose actions and present us to the outside world. The pathways that are used get stronger; those that are under-used grow weak and are eventually replaced."

Margie Meacham, an expert in the field of education and learning, known as "the Brain Lady".

Think about your brain as a muscle! Consistent practice and exposure to new challenges can create new pathways that make your brain more potent and intelligent.

Let's flip the coin. Do not see yourself as a failure as you have got to fail to succeed. Look to other people who have achieved. The evidence is all around you if only you choose to look and believe.

Remember, I shared my story in Chapter One about how I wanted to become a teacher, went to teacher training college, and did not complete that degree. I had another door of opportunity open for me and I went to live in the UK. Now I had a choice. I could have viewed that experience as a failure and focused on those damning negative thoughts that would have seen me slip into depression and hopelessness. Instead, I chose to see what other opportunities would present themselves.

Serving others seemed to be my destiny. I remembered that my dad wanted me to become a nurse. He believed that nurses worked hard and were very caring. He came to this thought after being ill and cared for by the nurses in the hospital.

At this time, I longed to become a lawyer, a yearning that never left me. Respecting and honouring parents' decisions are embedded as part of my culture. Therefore, at that time, I was happy to fulfil my dad's wishes and decided to take up the gauntlet of becoming a nurse, which led to me becoming a midwife, a field I still work in today. Remember, when one door closes for whatever reason, many more doors will present themselves to you to walk through.

You may find this concept a challenge, but you need to believe it to be true. You need courage and a willingness to accept that there may be a different path for you to walk. No matter the obstacles you may face, know and understand your choice of mindset links to your purpose, resulting in choosing the path of least resistance to achieve your dream and goals with ease and grace.

The actor Jim Carrey is a global superstar. He had a tough start in life and left school to find work so he could take care of his family. Despite this responsibility at a young age (15), Jim dreamed of becoming a comedian. His positive thinking and visualisation were the force he needed to achieve his vision. Today, Jim Carey is a devout believer in a positive mindset and talks about the power of affirmations. These are statements that you tell yourself and adopt as if you are that person who holds strong beliefs. He says that nothing in this world happens without a thought and intention behind it. His philosophy today and faith in his affirmations have made him a global celebrity.

It's your turn...

Here are some affirmations that you may use. Once you get the hang of it, you can create your own.

◊   I am worthy

◊   I am enough

◊   I am love

◊   I am strong

◊   I am determined

◊   I am successful

◊   I am prosperous

◊   I am...

◊   I am...

◊   I am...

*"**Believe you can achieve anything
as long as your mind is in it!**"*

Aunty Kate

You will achieve when you believe you can do it; that is a well-documented statement. Once you believe, you have to trust yourself. You have to work hard to achieve it. Saying it alone won't make it happen. Nothing changes without action.

Take a young child learning to walk. At the time of publication, my grandson is learning to walk. He keeps going. He looks out for ways to support his walk. He reaches out for the table to support him and enable him to keep edging forward. He instinctively finds a solution. He takes risks, he lets go, sometimes falling down but immediately getting back up whether he is encouraged. He is fostering intrinsic motivation to keep going. He knows what he wants to do and keeps going until he succeeds.

You are no different today as an adult than you were as a child. The difference is that your upbringing, culture and community have forced their limiting beliefs onto you, and in turn, you have adopted them as your truth; they are limiting beliefs and false.

One negative thought can divert your positive mind, and before long, you focus on the one negative thought and forget about all the positive experiences and ideas that are part of your learning. Remember, your mind is malleable, so if you focus on negative thoughts, you get more of the same; why not focus on the positive instead? You will be delighted with the results.

It's time to turn your attention to your thoughts and, more importantly, the words you use. Your language tells the tale of your thoughts. The words you use reveal what you think and your beliefs and, more importantly, serve as a signal to your inner being.

When you change your words, you change your mindset. When you face challenges, the table on the following page shows you how to change your words into a growth mindset statement!

INSTEAD OF...	TRY THINKING...
I'm not good at...	What am I missing...?
I give up	I'll try a different way
It's good enough	Is this my best work?
I can't make this any better	I can always improve
I made a mistake	Mistakes help me learn
I simply can't do it	I am going to train my brain
I'll never be that smart	I will learn how to do this
My friend can do it	I will learn from others

Your upbringing plays a large part in whether you develop negative thought patterns and negative mind chatter and words, or positive thought patterns creating encouraging mind chatter and comments. Remember, neuroscience has shown that the more you think negatively, the more likely you are to be negative and use fixed mindset

Dr Masaru Emoto, a Japanese scientist, was a pioneer in water study for over 20 years, and he *claimed* that environment, thoughts and emotions shape water. You will find his work documented in the New York Times bestseller, *The Hidden Messages in Water*. His experiments show water exposed to kind and pleasant thoughts resulted in aesthetically pleasing physical molecular formations in the water, while water exposed to fearful and discordant human intentions resulted in disconnected, disfigured and "unpleasant" physical molecular constructions. He carried out these experiments through Magnetic Resonance Analysis technology and high-speed photographs.

By using phrases such as "I love you", "thank you", and "you make me sick", he showed the difference in the formation of each water crystal.

Dr Masaru Emoto also claimed that music could affect the formation of the water crystals by using heavy metal and classical music. His work divides people – some accept his claims, whilst others feel there is not enough hard evidence behind the pseudo-science.

Train yourself to become more mindful of the words you are thinking of and using when talking to yourself or others. Here are five things to consider:

1. The Power of Words – be aware of your comments and try to change them.

2. Stop using the word No as this creates stress chemicals. Try saying YES more instead.

3. Intentionally choose to be positive – your mind responds more favourable to positivity as it is less threatened.

4. Create new brain connections – add the word "yet" to negative statements, e.g. "I can't solve this problem... yet!" When you add this small yet powerful word, it opens the door to possibilities.

5. Surround yourself with positive people – like attracts like, and it will raise your ability to solve problems by taking risks and considering how you say YES and commit to the necessary action to succeed.

Let me tell you a story...

When I came to England from Nigeria, I married my husband and settled into a new life. I also became a midwife and mother to four gorgeous children. Life was good until tragedy struck. I suddenly lost my husband, and I found myself with four children, the youngest being 18 months, to bring up alone. It was a difficult time. I was a mother, father, midwife, homemaker, and more. How would I bring them up by myself without parents and siblings around me? All my family were back in Nigeria.

After a short spell of grief, I had to make a decision: either to pick myself up and get on with things, or just rot. Being responsible for four lives made my decision easy. I got on with it. Three months later, I was back at work, bringing new life into the world. It was tough, but the negativity soon weakened by flexing my positive mindset. Being positive helps you carry on, and I believe I could do it. I looked to other single mothers who have carried on. The world is full of these heroes. I chose not to think about how life had treated me, as that would be my downfall. My drive was to move on and be a role model for many less fortunate mothers who needed my strength and guidance.

An open mind

A positive mindset is an open mind, which means you are open to possibilities. As the fabulous Audrey Hepburn once said, "Nothing is impossible. The word itself says I'm Possible."

Being open-minded means creating space in your mind to achieve other things. In my forties, I finally got to fulfil my dream of becoming a lawyer. Even if I had failed, I would have used my open-mindedness to accept the failure and find a different route.

When you adopt an open-minded approach, opportunities come your way. When you have a closed mind, you only focus on one thing: failure. Choosing to always focus on the positive resulted in me exploring where I had failed and what else I could do to ensure success. Being open-minded means you are prepared to accept what comes to you. Achieving your goal may come in a way that you do not expect; and it may come from conversations, reading or watching TV. When these ideas flood your mind, they can create the spark to try something new or different...

"Open-minded people embrace being wrong,
are free of illusions,
don't mind what people think of them,
and question everything, even themselves."

Anon

Being open-minded allows you to think about things differently. You take it step by step and may have to accept the changes that may arise during that path. It is about finding solutions. Too many people focus on their problems. When you adopt this thinking, it exacerbates negative mind patterns, but when you challenge yourself to think more openly, ideas can spark new ways of thinking and behaviours. When you focus on the possibilities and give them a try, you will often be surprised at how easy you achieve what you set out to do. Just 1% of negative thoughts can diminish 99% of positive reviews, so it is essential to keep positive.

The prestigious film director Steven Spielberg was rejected from film school three times. His persistence, determination and open mind kept him going because he believed that education was the path to success. His tenacity finally paid off when he was accepted into another school, only to then drop out to fulfil his dream of becoming a director. His open mind knew that there was more than one way to achieve his dream.

Nonetheless, 35 years later, Spielberg returned to school to complete his work and earn his BA.

> "**When you open your mind,**
> **you open the door to endless possibilities.**"
> **Aunty Kate**

A flexible mind

A flexible mind will not give up, and it will look for alternative ways of achieving what it wants. It believes that ideas are not fixed, but instead, improvement is possible with more trying and learning. A person with a flexible mind will find a way to make it happen for them.

I demonstrated flexibility of thought after completing my law degree. I wanted to go straight into practice, but I had to be flexible because doubt crossed my mind that I may not have liked law but instead maintained my preference for midwifery. I soon found a way to combine my law and midwifery practice, and I explored how I could use the two together. By being flexible and not having to decide between the two areas of law and medicine, I knew that reflecting on my experience would provide the answer. Sure enough, sometimes mistakes occurred at the hospital, which led to litigation. If I could combine my midwifery and new law degree, I could monitor this aspect of my work within the hospital. This whole process enabled me to venture into the field of medical negligence. It meant I could work within the department, scrutinise the notes when complaints were made, and see where and how we could improve the service. Being flexible allowed me to maintain practising my midwifery and incorporating my legal knowledge.

I became the Royal College of Midwives Steward, where I used my law knowledge to support my colleagues. It opened many doors of opportunity too. Having a law degree provided the opportunity to work more in the community and support people with housing, social services and environmental support. I could signpost my clients to what they needed, and my law degree enabled me to do that with ease. It also paved the path to politics.

"Being flexible in thought allows you to
achieve beyond your expectation
and provides new pathways and ideas
to solutions and success."

Aunty Kate

A conscious mind

When you are conscious, you are aware of yourself and the world around you. Please wake up and become familiar and turn it towards your inner being. Self-awareness is an aspect of emotional intelligence, suggesting that reflections provide an opportunity to self-assess. Self-assessment is a challenging task because it asks you to be completely honest with yourself and that introspection takes courage. May I remind you that courage is the first step to change? Learn to become aware of your inner resources, abilities and limits.

When you recognise and use these competencies, you are:

◊   Aware of your strengths and weaknesses

◊   Reflective and learn from experience

◊   Open to honest feedback, new perspectives, continuous learning and self-development

◊   Able to show a sense of humour and perspective about yourself

Many people go through life in an unconsciousness state, much like your unconscious mind controls your breathing, heart rate and digestion. You consciously do not tell your body to do these vital tasks, like switching on a light. The more conscious you are of your thoughts, actions and perspectives, the more you can take control and change them so as to learn and grow.

Let me share a story...

The Teacup

There was once a well-educated, highly successful man who visited a Zen master to ask for solutions to his problems. As the Zen master and the man conversed, the man would frequently interrupt the Zen master to interject his own beliefs, not allowing the Zen master to finish many sentences.

Finally, the Zen master stopped talking and offered the man a cup of tea. When the Zen master poured the tea, he kept running after the cup was full, causing it to overflow.

"Stop pouring," the man said. "The cup is full."

The Zen master stopped and said, "Similarly, you are too full of your own opinions. You want my help, but you have no room in your cup to receive my words."

Moral of the story:

This Zen story is a reminder that your beliefs are not you. When you unconsciously hold on to your ideas, you become rigid and closed-mind to learn and expand your consciousness. The path to self-realisation is to stay conscious of your beliefs and always be open to learning.

Your mind loves metaphors and stories. You can begin to create change in your subconscious mind through metaphor as it tries to understand the meaning. Your conscious mind's job is to know what is happening within and around you.

Developing control of your mind gives you power over your life.

> *"Your mind is a powerful thing.*
> *When you fill it with positive thoughts,*
> *your life will change."*
>
> **Buddha**

Aunty Kate's Learning Points

◊ Develop a growth mindset.

◊ Accept mistakes and failures as opportunities to learn.

◊ Adopt the power of affirmations.

◊ Change your negative thoughts and words into positive ones.

◊ Be open-minded to possibilities.

◊ Be flexible in your thoughts – look for the 'yes' and solutions.

◊ Be conscious – become more aware of yourself and the world around you.

One last thing...

Achieving your goals takes courage and a strong mindset. Understanding your perspective and how you can strengthen your mindset is vital to success in all aspects of life. Exploring Dr Carol Dweck's two types of mindset – Fixed and Growth – provides the invaluable insight you need to develop your growth mindset for happiness and success in life. Through my life experiences, I have demonstrated the power of the mind and that it is you who needs to take responsibility and make the necessary changes.

Kate as a student nurse

Chapter Three: Motivation

Visions, Goals, and Missions

"I hate every minute of training. But I said, 'Don't quit. Suffer now and live the rest of your life as a champion.'"
Muhammad Ali,
American heavyweight boxer and activist,
known as "The Greatest"

What is motivation?

According to the Oxford English Dictionary, motivation is:
a reason for acting or behaving in a particular way.

Online magazine *Psychology Today* describes motivation as a driving force fuelling human behaviour, sparking competition and igniting social connections. The magazine suggests that having no motivation could lead to mental illnesses, including depression. I believe cause embraces the longing to be determined to finding meaning, purpose, and a life worth living.

Types of motivation

There are two types of motivation: Extrinsic and Intrinsic. As humans, we are motivated by both types, but the power lies in igniting intrinsic motivation as it ignites from within ourselves. Discovering intrinsic motivation needs the courage to connect within and reignite the passion that once blazed inside of you as a child. The sustainable driving force will see you through tricky times no matter what. With intention, your desire to succeed rises above all the challenges and obstacles you may face along the way. It is vital to connect within and know what fires up the energy and life within you.

Extrinsic motivation

Sportsmen and women – such as Christine Ijeoma Ohuruogu, 400-metre athlete; Sir Mo Farah, Somalian-born British distance runner; and Serena Williams, one of the most decorated female tennis players – are all driven. They prime themselves to win Olympic gold medals, world titles and other awards that recognise their brilliance and talent. They have learned not to let failure, age or race stand in their way of achievement; instead, they use it to fuel their determination, grit and commitment to succeed.

Serena Williams' success story in the tennis world is unprecedented in the modern open era. At the 'tender' age of 40, she continues to be driven by breaking records. In 2021, she strove to match the number of wins in major titles (24) currently held (at the time of writing this book) by Margaret Court. Williams does not simply rely on being motivated from the outside by achieving great accolades; this is also infused by the intrinsic motivation to be the best and compete against herself and other champion competitors. Despite injuries, facing the media pack and having a baby that almost cost her life, Serena's strong mindset was the catalyst to continue. Furthermore, her commitment to returning to physical health and drive to continue to play the sport that she loves is a testimony to what it takes to become a world-class champion.

Most of us are not world-class champions, but we are champions nonetheless. By looking to others who have achieved something you desire, you can find something in them that you want to emulate. Consider qualities such as purpose, mindset and motivation driving you, despite or even because of the challenges you may face. Winning take grit, commitment and determination to succeed.

It's your turn...

Think back to when you achieved something because someone else wanted you to do what they considered 'best' for you. Consider how and what external rewards affected your behaviour. Perhaps you remember your parents saying something like, "If you clean your room, you can get those new trainers you want." A cultural, community and societal limitation is conditioning to achieve small everyday tasks and challenges with an external reward from a young age.

Once in the education system, you begin sitting exams for a certificate to enable you to go onto the next level of your life. You require certification for entry into university, securing a job, or succeeding in a training course. Sadly, choices and decisions exclude what lights you up inside but are more likely to be on external expectations.

The danger of extrinsic motivation is that you become a people-pleaser. You remain unfulfilled or walk a path that does not lead you to live your dream or help you find your purpose.

It is not all bad, as extrinsic motivation has its place in your life, but it does not trump living a life motivated from within. That is where your true power lies to achieve whatever goals you set yourself.

Intrinsic motivation

The American author Daniel Pink argues that we think motivation is either motivated by a fear of punishment or the excitement of a reward. Of course, he describes the extrinsic motivation, but he believes we are inspired and best served by three other forces of intrinsic motivation: autonomy, mastery, and purpose.

Autonomy is the need to self-direct.

Mastery is the intrinsic motivation to get better, to master a skill.

Purpose is the ability to connect to a more significant cause.

And, according to Pink, it's the highest form of motivation.

Understanding this concept provides you with the knowledge that there is a process you go through from autonomy to purpose where intrinsic motivation drives you, no matter what obstacles or challenges you may face in life. You begin to accept this more as you delve deeper into who you are and work on the goal of being better today than yesterday. Intrinsic motivation at the mastery level is all about self-improvement, so there is never a need to compare or be competitive with anyone else. You are your competition.

Before sharing my experience, I would like to mention a strong black Nigerian woman I admire Ngozi Okonjo-Iweala is the first black African woman to become the Director-General of the World Trade Organization. She was born into academia and surrounded by knowing the value of education. She knows the power of learning, applying newly gained knowledge and skills, and using it to serve others and make a difference.

Her story illustrates her commitment to her chosen field as an economist. She served for 25 years in the World Bank in Washington DC, serving her country twice as Nigeria's Finance Minister and Minister of Foreign Affairs. As a futurist, Okonjo-Iweala has been part of UNESCO's International Commission on the Futures of Education. She has been able to shape the future for younger generations to come with her philosophy, voice and vision.

Her story is truly remarkable, for her love and commitment to her chosen field have catapulted her into being recognised for her accomplishments, gifts and talents. Reflect on how and what she achieved and find what traits she has demonstrated; these are the life lessons you must heed.

I would like to share my story as an ordinary Nigerian woman about how my intrinsic motivation has enabled me to achieve the best outcomes in my life.

As mentioned in Chapter 2, when I reached my forties, I finally was able to fulfil my dream of becoming a lawyer. What's important is that if you have an intense desire and plan, it does not matter how long it takes to achieve it; believe that you will when the time is right. I want to share a deeper aspect of how I overcame many challenges due to keeping my eye on my goal. I had a vision linked to my purpose of being a great family lawyer serving vulnerable women in my community.

One of the lecturers asked me about my current situation at my interview. I was a single mother of four children, working full-time as a midwife and was one of the team leaders in the maternity unit at the hospital. They wondered how I would juggle all of these things at the same time, given my commitments. They explained that the degree I had applied for was one of the most cognitively challenging courses, requiring time, dedication and commitment.

Of course, the thought of being told 'NO' was not in my field of vision, and I had already proven that once I set my mind to something, the only path to choose is the one that leads to success. Focused, determined and driven to achieve this lifelong dream, I overcame anything that stood in my way. I did whatever I needed to do to hold that degree in my hand.

I left that meeting knowing I had two weeks to consider my position. During this time, I had to consider my options, particularly around childcare. I have to say it is during these times that you grit your teeth as you need to dig deep, be vulnerable and ask for help. You will never know what you can achieve if you allow pride, doubt and worthlessness to block your possibilities. I was surrounded and blessed with many good, non-judgemental friends who were only too happy to help me achieve my dream.

> *"I don't count my sit-ups;*
> *I only start counting when it starts hurting*
> *because they're the only ones that count."*
> **Muhammed Ali**

From my story, it is clear that my drive links to the intrinsic motivation of fulfilling a dream and vision related to my purpose of becoming a great family lawyer, serving vulnerable women in my community.

When you listen to your inner voice and follow your heart, the answers and opportunities to succeed magically appear before you. You believe in yourself and visualise yourself doing what is, at one stage, a dream.

What does your inner voice say to you? Do you listen or silence it, believing it is impossible for you? You are the only one limiting yourself. Like all the other brilliant people whose stories I have shared with you, everything is possible when you begin to trust in yourself and follow that dream. We all know our purpose when we choose to connect within and hear the voice of wisdom that is our birthright.

The importance of having a vision

A vision is something bigger than you that you want to achieve in the future – the bigger the dream, the better the drive. It allows you to look forward to the end. One of the necessary ingredients is self-discipline which is vital to moving forward as you take small steps each day towards your vision. Consider yourself the master of your destiny; think of yourself as the ringmaster encouraging you to reach your vision each day.

"Your vision is limited only by you.
See yourself as the truly capable human being
that you are."

Dr Moses Simuyemba,
Doctor, author and speaker
known as "Africa's Success Coach"

Let me tell you a story...

When I arrived in England from Nigeria, I had a vision of becoming a nurse to fulfil my father's wish for me. I used to see the nurses and visualised myself in that role. But it was a more significant role, not just as a staff nurse but as a Sister in charge of the ward.

Once you establish a clear vision, you can set about how you will carry out your mission, which is related to your idea and driven by your values. It ignites the passion and motivation within you to succeed, overcome challenges and strengthen your resilience.

Of course, life is never simple, and often, hurdles are placed in our path. At this time, I was married, looking after my husband and baby.

I soon learned that it was necessary to juggle everything to achieve my vision. When you make such a firm decision, you need to practise self-discipline each day. Fuelling my drive was determination, as I needed this in spades to rise above the challenges I faced. One of the main challenges was that I now lived in a new country, where I had to acclimatise to the cold weather, build new relationships, and get used to the environment.

As each day passed, my goal grew into the same vision as my father's wish, and I made it my mission to become a nurse.

Goal setting

How do you eat an elephant? The answer is – one bite at a time. It can become overwhelming when you have an audacious vision if you do not break it down into small bite-sized pieces. We call these bite-size pieces GOALS. Perceive your intents as the small tasks lead to a bigger vision. It is essential to learn how to set achievable goals that allow you to keep moving forward and growing.

What is goal setting?

Goal setting is a robust process that allows you to think about something you want in your future. The goals you set also motivate you to turn your vision of this future into reality.

Setting goals helps you choose where you want to go in life. By precisely knowing what you want to achieve, you know what you have to focus on and where you have to concentrate your efforts. You'll also quickly spot the distractions that can so easily lead you astray.

The importance of goal setting

If you do not write down your goals, they are said to remain just dreams. By committing pen to paper (or typing!), there is an added energy and compelling desire to achieve them. Some people see this as ticking off their list, and it can provide a sense of accomplishment.

In turn, it continues to generate intrinsic motivation to keep going even when things get tough.

Many people set SMART goals. Using this helpful mnemonic makes your goals more powerful. SMART goals are:

Specific

Measurable

Attainable

Relevant

Timed

For example, instead of having "to climb Mount Everest" as a goal, it's more powerful to use the SMART goal: "To have climbed to the top of Mount Everest by December 31, 2027." The goal will only be attainable with detailed preparation.

- When you set your big goal, the next part of the process is to break it down into smaller steps. Doing so will allow you to take the necessary steps one at a time to attain your goal.

- Use positive language and affirmations such as "I will climb to the top with ease."

- Precision is key. Include dates, times and amounts so you can measure your success.

- Prioritise. Order your goals in their level of importance. Organising your goals helps you avoid feeling overwhelmed by having too many goals. Now you can give attention to each one and tick them off.

- Write your goals down. The physical writing of your goals gives them energy, and you are more likely to take action.

- Keep the goals small. The goals must be relevant and achievable, so do not make them too big that you get overwhelmed and feel less motivated to achieve them. Instead of a goal such as "buy equipment for the climb," you could state, "buy climbing boots by [date]" and so on.

- Set realistic goals. The small goals you set should be achievable in a short timescale, which will keep you motivated. Climbing

Mount Everest is a big audacious goal, so something realistic in preparation might be to climb a minor hill or mountain to build up your stamina and skill.

Let me tell you a story...

As a locally elected councillor, I want to show you how to use SMART goals for planning purposes that enable you to achieve the target of being elected. First of all, the politicians from each party will hold a meeting to create a **Specific** plan of attack; one of the actions is to set up their manifesto to help the voters decide who to vote for. Next, they find a way to **Measure** how many local communities will vote for them. Then they have an idea of what is possible for them to **Attain**. They have to ensure that each task is **Relevant** to gaining voters' votes. Lastly, they will know that they have a **Time** period of six weeks to put their plan of action into practice.

As they journey along with their plan, they can reflect and tweak goals and learn from the experience.

Aunty Kate's Learning Points

◊   Create a vision for your life. Consider your role model; think about what you love to do, and take time out to daydream about how you see yourself in that role.

◊   Look for evidence around you. Consider those who have already achieved what you are envisioning.

◊   Ensure that you link to something you are passionate about and use this energy to keep you driven and motivated.

◊   Find a mission and commit to it, no matter what. It has to be something bigger than yourself and relate to your Vision and Passion.

◊   Set goals, one step at a time, to keep you always focused on the prize, allowing you to smash any challenges that get in your way.

◊   Continue to believe in yourself and strengthen your resilience. It took 10,000 attempts to develop a light bulb before Edison experienced success.

◊   There is no such thing as failure, only learning.

One Last Thing...

Motivation fuelled by a strong 'why' ignites powerful intrinsic motivation, sustaining your persistence in reaching your goals. When you adopt Daniel Pink's suggestion of Autonomy, Mastery and Purpose as the driving power to achieve, you accept that progress and success are your responsibility. It's vital to create a vision for your life, including what you choose to do day in and day out. Write down your SMART goals and commit to taking positive action each day and deepen your confidence. Find role models and mentors you look up to as evidence that everything is possible. Above all, believe in yourself and strengthen your resilience by knowing that failure is part of success.

Chapter Four:
Faith

Acceptance, Trust, God, Humanity

"To one who has faith, no explanation is necessary.
To one without faith, no explanation is possible."
St Thomas Aquinas
Italian priest, philosopher, theologian

What is faith?

According to the Oxford English Dictionary, faith is:

complete trust or confidence in someone or something.

It is essential to have faith in yourself if you want to achieve. It's about having confidence and trust in yourself and what you do or want to do. When you have a child, you believe your toddler will learn to walk and talk; as a grandparent, I watch my grandchild learn to walk. As he tries to lift his leg, you can see the uncertainty as he looks around, wondering where he should place it. As soon as he's stronger, he develops faith and belief that he can do it, allowing himself to lift his leg forward. Now we can celebrate and clap when he's done it. This interaction strengthens a child's faith in trying new things as part of their development.

As you grow and develop, you begin to believe in processes. Soon you think that with practice, you can achieve any skill such as riding a bike, playing the piano or learning to drive. When you falter along the way, you either allow the setbacks to lessen your faith, or use them to build confidence and assurance that you will achieve the goal.

With faith, you often have to put it into the hands of another person. You cannot control everything in your life, so you depend upon others for many aspects of living. When you are pregnant, you have faith that medical professionals will help you deliver your baby safely. Consider the midwife's confidence in her studies that what she learns will enable her to bring a new life into this world, even when complications arise during the birth. Every time you step on a plane, you have faith that the pilot will fly everyone safely to their destination.

Faith is something you have within you. It cannot be seen or touched but it is a feeling or a thought that guides you in life, allowing you to trust yourself and others confidently.

Faith has played a significant part in my life. As previously mentioned, I found myself widowed with four children ranging in age from 12 years to 18 months. Devastated at my husband's death, I could not afford to crumble because I was now solely responsible for their upbringing and well-being.

Despite having lived in the UK for more than 12 years, I still felt uneasy about having the proper support around me to help with my childcare needs and growing family. Making good friends was not that easy, but if I had not dug deep inside and held onto my faith that God would provide what I needed, my life would be different today.

Another way I decided to strengthen my faith was to throw myself into the church's work. I believed that serving God through helping others would be the way to achieve my social needs and fortify my spirituality and relationship with the Almighty. I have learned that when you face challenges, one solution is to help others with their struggles, and this provides you with reinforced strength and outlook that enables you to cope better with your problems.

When you connect with your faith, you can be vulnerable and share your story, which helps others review and strengthen their faith. One of the life lessons I have learned is to show kindness to others.

You never know what other people are struggling with, and those who have big smiles can often be the ones who are suffering the most.

Adopting positive action and responsibility for my faith and family made me feel blessed with the gift of friendship and support from other people like me within the church. It reinforced the trust and belief in the sincerity of their actions towards me and my children. My faith and the people I met in the church galvanised my confidence in being able to keep going and achieve my goals for the sake of my children. The ripple effect of this experience has impacted and influenced not just me but also my children as they too made so many new friends and learnt to socialise and interact with other families, building their confidence and building their belief in the importance of community.

The faith inside you gives you the courage to change, step outside of your comfort zone and venture into new beginnings. When you trust in your faith, you can move forward with confidence, grow and achieve goals way beyond what you think is possible.

While life can be hard at the darkest of times, faith is a sense of knowing deep down inside that things will get better.

Acceptance

Acceptance is a difficult concept for humans to achieve. Many people hold on to grudges, bitterness and guilt, which hurt them. Facing this hurt takes courage, and that is the most crucial decision to make but somehow, even in their pain, they decide to keep picking the scab instead of facing the fear.

There are times when you feel let down by others. You have trusted them, and they have let you down and broken your confidence. When this happens, it becomes a challenge for some people to accept even an apology. In my experience, I have found that particularly women in my community can sometimes tell lies to protect themselves and others from knowing something less favourable about them. These women want to be seen as the 'good' ones and not someone who creates chaos and division.

It becomes a game of ping-pong with 'he said/ she said' illustrating childish traits and behaviour. They enter a 'blame' game rather than take responsibility for their thoughts, words and actions, digging deeper.

When people resort to behaviours that demonstrate a fear of being judged, it causes them to lie. This attitude can make something relatively simple become as complicated as unravelling the truth, like a plate of spaghetti. Like Chinese whispers in a group of friends, a statement can easily be infused with exaggerations of the truth, and before you know it, someone has a finger pointing at them. Imagine a young person blamed by the community for breaking into a house when someone used the wrong name along the chain. Such tittle-tattle stories create much pain for the subject when they are untrue. It is always best to tell the truth and accept that you are not perfect in these situations. Honesty often needs you to be vulnerable, act with courage and gain respect, even if you do something deemed wrong.

Accepting failure

An area where we can all relate is passing exams or tests. As children at school, examinations are par for the course early on in life. The world we live in focuses on exams to select the 'best' brains, skill sets and aptitude for various subjects.

In 2019, a third of young people failed their GCSEs in English and maths, causing headteachers to call for change. The education system continues to try and put square pegs into round holes as people have a range of talents and gifts that are not simply academic. Failing is not what is important; it is in developing the mindset of people to realise that failure is part of success.

In 2019-2020, 37% of students at university were mature students. Many young people do not fit into the norm of schooling during their teenage years, and it is not until later in life, after many trials and tribulations, that they find the path they want to take in life. There is a saying "Where there is a will, there is a way", and for some, it is when they take control of their lives rather than being told what they must do that success comes more easily to them.

Take the world-famous Walt Disney. He dropped out of art school at a young age, and it wasn't until his thirties that he decided to go back and achieve the degree he had started many years before.

Always know there is hope. Simply because you may not have achieved at school does not mean you cannot succeed in life, because once you align yourself with who you are, then the *Time for Purpose* emerges. Remember that as you journey through life, you meet different people who negatively impact your life. You soon learn to surround yourself with like-minded people who understand the need for failure to grow.

Consider one of these three great people: Sir Richard Branson, Albert Einstein and J.K. Rowling. These famous people faced hardship, confusion and failure before achieving worldwide acclaimed fame. Branson is famously known as being a person with dyslexia. Einstein gave his mother a note from school which read, "Your son is a genius. This school is too small for him and doesn't have enough good teachers for training him. Please teach him yourself." J.K. Rowling was once an impoverished single mother living on benefits. These stories around famous people are the evidence you need to inspire and motivate you into action, knowing that all things are possible with time, determination and effort. All of these people and more learn to accept that failure is par for the course of success.

It's your turn...

Consider a time in your life when you were successful. What did you have to overcome? What failures did you make? And what were the lessons from those failures that allowed you to pick yourself up and achieve? Now think of a famous person you admire... find out what their story is and what they did to achieve their success. What failures did they overcome?

Let me tell you a story...

Most people will learn to drive, a skill that takes time, effort and commitment. Have you passed your driving test? How many times did you try before you succeeded? Let me tell you about my driving story. As a high achiever, I expected to pass my driving test the first time. Alas, it was not to be. It took me three attempts before I finally passed my test! Having failed twice before did not deter me from getting that vital piece of paper that said I passed!

I also had to consider the investment and cost of all the required lessons to pass my test. As I had invested money in learning to drive, it also fuelled my drive (no pun intended!) to keep going and work doubly hard to ensure I practised with my husband to cut down the expense of this much-needed goal.

I turned my focus to thinking about what being able to drive would mean for me rather than thinking about the test itself. This change in mindset was the catalyst I needed to ensure I achieved my goal. So instead, I thought about being able to take my children to school, family days out and how I would save time travelling around in my additional agency work as a midwife, as often I would have to travel quite a distance between jobs.

> *"God grant me the serenity to accept the things*
> *I cannot change, courage to change the things I can,*
> *and wisdom to know the difference."*
>
> **St Francis of Assisi**
> **one of the most venerated religious figures in Christianity**

Trust

With faith comes trust. Trust is when you believe in the reliability, truth or ability of someone or something. As humans, when you feel betrayed or let down, trust breaks. Once trust is lost, to regain it feels like climbing Mount Everest.

Let's consider trusting ourselves. We often go about our business and don't consciously think about whether we trust ourselves or not. We tend to believe that we will do the 'right' thing. Most of your behaviour is triggered from an unconscious level. When you become aware of a negative pattern, such as lying, cheating or addiction to drugs, alcohol or sex, you wake up and begin to take notice of the detrimental impact this way of living has on your life. You are more likely to say, "I do not trust myself around alcohol." Mistrust opens the door to failure because you no longer try to achieve anything and prefer to live in a downward spiral. This negative perception is false, but it's the behaviour in question. At every moment, you have the power and choice to choose differently. As the saying goes, "it is never too late".

At the ripe young age of 43, I decided to study law. In 1992, not too many older single people with four children went to university to learn, let alone a very demanding law degree. But I had faith in my ability and a drive to achieve a long-standing goal; therefore, I trusted that I could do it and focus on each step one day at a time. Compounding the challenge further was that I was still practising midwifery full-time.

Consider the people in your life: some are in it for a short time, some for a reason, and some for a season. Learning this about people will take you down a path to why they are part of your life. When you explore some of the reasons, you also become aware that some of these people are good for you, support you and want you to achieve. In contrast, others only seem to criticise, discourage, and be unhelpful when you want to move forward, especially if it is a challenging task.

Often in my life, people judged me when I took on other responsibilities along with my career as a midwife. I sidestepped this issue by focusing on what I did rather than sharing it with some of my friends. It was easier than listening to their negativity. My energy fuelled the focus on succeeding, not arguing my case when my mind had already been made up. You will undoubtedly be able to see yourself in this scenario and consider whether you are an encouraging friend who accepts and nurtures others. Perhaps you may see yourself as one of the discouraging friends who always questions, judges and comments on other people's lives.

Of course, to balance this, I had friends I could trust and knew would still be by my side no matter what I chose to do. When it comes to trusting friends, you need to be wise, diligent and listen to your inner voice's intuition.

Trust is fragile, and many scorned people experience difficulty rebuilding trust after it has gone. One of the most impactful ways of dealing with a lack of faith is to learn how to forgive. Again, this is not easy to do, but it will save you many years of heartache and disillusionment.

When you learn to forgive others, it does not mean that what they have done is okay, but it does release you and negative emotions from being like a yoke around your neck throughout life. Forgiveness means letting someone or some misdemeanour go, enabling you to move on in your life. This work is deep-rooted and aligns with your values. Once you understand this process, you are free to go forward and learn to put your trust in others again. This time though, you will be able to identify the red flags that tell you some people are not worthy of your trust.

Let me tell you a story…

A devout merchant drove his Mercedes hundreds of miles across the Arabian deserts to worship with the Holy Man. When he arrived, he parked his car outside the simple lodging and entered to embark on a week of study. He fasted, meditated and prayed for seven days and nights, fully surrendering himself to the power of Almighty God.

But when he looked for his car afterwards, he discovered it was no longer where he had left it. He searched everywhere, but his Mercedes was nowhere to be seen. He complained bitterly to the Holy Man. "Look how I have been let down, and I have spent days and nights worshipping and see how God treats me!"

The Holy Man smiled and said, "Trust in God and tie your camel securely."

Traditional Oriental tale

This metaphor illustrates that people should take responsibility to achieve a good outcome and then trust God or the universe that this will happen.

God and humanity

Being born into a Christian family has significantly impacted me. Both my parents were great believers in God, and their lives reflected the Christian way of life. They set me an excellent example of how to live a good life. One of the valuable rituals we participated in was prayer, and we prayed in the morning, at mealtimes and in the evening.

There are particular words that we say in our heads that enable us to believe that those prayers are the ones that guide you in life and lead you to achieve. My parents had a choice, and they decided to bring me and my siblings up in the way of the Christian Church. They believed that this would create a loving and happy future for their children, who would live a good life and help within the society.

My parents always took us to church, where we could be part of a community of like-minded people who lived by the same guidelines. Attending church developed a strong sense of belonging, which resulted in us attending many clubs, groups and church programmes. A clear focus on bettering ourselves and volunteering for charitable works within the community guided us to choose what was right rather than become involved in antisocial behaviour. I liked to help the elderly and play sports, such as netball, with the youth teams.

This upbringing has served me immensely throughout my life, and it has provided a solid foundation that has helped me cope with losing a baby (see Chapter Six for more insight), widowhood, and studies as a mature student. Every time I faced a challenge, I prayed and prayed, resulting in an inner strength that allowed me to carry on through motivation and an innate need to succeed.

Let me lay my cards on the table: I would like to share with you that although I am a high achiever who has a strong belief in God, there are times when as a human, I question some of the behaviours of others, especially within my culture of being a Nigerian woman.

Within the Igbo culture of Eastern Nigeria, when a husband dies and leaves a widow, she is blamed. When my beloved husband was suddenly taken from this life, I was fortunate to live in the UK; however, it did not stop my husband's family from blaming me. If you find yourself in a similar situation, you need to do two things.

Firstly, be brave and find the courage to create the change you desire. Secondly, value education, for it is the key to freedom. Take action and learn all you can about what you are passionate about and live your life using it to fuel your purpose.

My message to you is that you do not have to be a Christian to lead a good life, but you do need to believe in something, and more importantly, you need to believe in yourself. Having faith in something is the most significant investment you can make during your life. Learn to nurture yourself, learn every day, give thanks for what you have, and leave all else that does not serve you to float away, leaving you with a feeling of peace inside.

Aunty Kate's Learning Points...

◊   Believe in yourself first before you have faith in anyone else.

◊   With faith comes trust and confidence, so always trust yourself.

◊   Faith ignites the courage to take action for change.

◊   Acceptance is vital as it enables you to be vulnerable, especially when you make mistakes, revealing your true power.

◊   Know what you can control and stick to that; control outside of you is none of your business.

◊   Learn to forgive; it will set you free.

◊   Put yourself first and nurture the faith in yourself; give thanks and let go of what does not serve you to become the best version of yourself each day.

One last thing...

When you do not believe or trust in yourself, you will find it challenging to believe and trust others around you. Nurturing faith and trust will free you from mistrust, uncertainty and bitterness. It's vital to your inner peace to learn to let go of what you cannot control, accept what is and allow yourself to be vulnerable without judgement. Find a power to believe in that is more significant than you, and watch how you will blossom without the weight of disbelief and mistrust around your neck. The greatest liberator of all is forgiveness. Believe and set your mind to do anything you want.

On Graduation Day

Kate in her Chieftaincy attire

Chapter Five: Drive

Determination, Willpower, Stamina

"Human beings have an innate inner drive to be autonomous, self-determined, and connected to one another. And when that drive is liberated, people achieve more and live richer lives."

Daniel Pink
American author and speaker

D o you leave the house with a full fuel tank for the day ahead, or do you always run on empty?

In today's world, we all seem to be rushing around and trying to achieve so much in one day. Living life too much in the fast lane leads to burnout. You feel depleted of energy, and it never seems to be replenished, no matter what you do. We often do not give ourselves the time to sit back, relax and chill. Time out is essential if you are to ensure your energy tank fills once again to take on the day and the world at your pace.

Consider transitioning into adulthood. When you are a child, you seem to have endless energy. Your life consists of playing and pleasure. A good work ethic develops from your education and experience, increasing intensity as you travel through your educational journey.

The work becomes more challenging; therefore, you need to take time from playing and pleasure and focus on your schoolwork.

Conserving and controlling your energy is not part of your daily routine. As a child, if you are tired, you fall asleep to refill your energy; this is a habit you lose in adulthood. You may have developed some limiting beliefs, such as adults do not generally doze during the day for fear of being labelled lazy. Perception and mindset play a significant role in your decision-making and perspective, depending on your experiences and childhood environment.

As you grow up, priorities change, and you soon learn that there is much to do in life. Go to work, keep a clean house, bring up a family, pay the bills and find time for socialising and last but not least, time for yourself. You cannot pour from an empty vessel. At times, everything becomes consuming and exhausting, and you realise that you cannot go on in the same way. Something has to change. You have to learn the skills involved in time management if you want to feel in control and less exhausted. Let's consider time management around travel.

Travelling for work and pleasure is a significant part of our daily lives. Therefore, learning to drive becomes necessary to enjoy more time doing what you love rather than using public transport to go from A to B.

Learning to drive allows you to go from A to B as quickly and efficiently as possible to make your life easier. Passing your driving test gives you the drive, determination and willpower to succeed. You do whatever it takes to ensure you gain your driver's licence. You hire a professional driving instructor, listen to and follow their instructions, and put in the practice so you can pass your driving test. With that result, you gain a licence and are free to drive wherever and whenever you want. It gives you a greater sense of freedom.

Applying the above logical process, your drive in life is the same in many situations. You have to set a goal, find support, learn the skills, and put in the time and action to achieve it. Be aware that your environment and experiences as a young person growing up impact and prepare you for life. You learn from many backgrounds, and you soon know what you like to do and become more aware of the things you choose to avoid. Earlier, we talked about the two types of motivation – intrinsic and extrinsic – closely linked to your drive. The aim is to foster intrinsic motivation so that you are in control of your success through making positive choices. Remember to use the analogy of learning to drive to remind what it takes to succeed.

In his article 'Developing Drive' in the magazine *Psychology Today*, Dr Marty Nemko suggests that most attempts to improve motivation and reduce procrastination focus on the analogy of the stick and the carrot. Consider the benefits and liabilities of doing the task: "You'll get a promotion; you won't get fired." Or there are reminders, such as calendars, scheduling, to-do lists, and check-ins which you can use. These are ways of keeping you motivated that rely more on extrinsic motivation as they are motivators outside of you.

Arguably, three elements affect you: your perception of the pursuit of happiness, unreasonable fear of failure, and actual fear of failure. It is beneficial to see happiness as a journey where you can choose a positive attitude, develop a good work ethic that harvests rewards, and learn to enjoy the process instead of focusing on the destination.

What is your perspective on failure? Is it something you avoid and keeps you in your comfort zone? Do you practice risk aversion? How will you know whether you like it if you do not try it? You may even discover that you are good at what you fear. With an unreasonable fear of failure, you remain stuck, and life seems to not go in your favour, and so you develop limiting beliefs around that which you fear. You will find yourself saying things like, "It never works out for me, so why should I bother? I'm not good at X; I'm not going even to try! I'm not going to ask them to the party because they will only say no." These remarks feed procrastination and lack of self-worth and lessen your confidence. But remember, there are always two sides to a coin.

Once you understand that failure is part of success, you begin to change your attitude to trying new things, meeting new people and believing that whatever you fear is possible. When you consider the different mindsets, you soon realise that a growth mindset is needed to fuel your drive. Therefore, it is essential to see failure as part of the road to success and not as something to judge, criticise or devalue yourself.

Imagine what your life would be like if you decided to change. Of course, change is one of the most challenging things in life, and it relies on breaking old habits and establishing new ones. In committing to change, you must consider your environment and surrounding people.

If you want to get healthy, stop smoking and drink less, but if you carry on going to the pub with friends, the environment itself will not help you reach your goals. Instead of going to the pub, you could choose to go for a walk, visit the gym, or swim. You will find yourself in these new environments that motivate you and improve your health. As a bonus, you will meet new like-minded friends with goals exactly like you.

It is the same for the people who surround you. For example, you may have friends who are always moaning and belittling others. This behaviour can be infectious, and you find yourself behaving in the same way. This behaviour and chit-chat causes you to feel unsettled as it does not reflect who you really are on the inside. When you choose to change, you need to surround yourself with positive vibes, which may mean breaking old relationships and forming new healthier ones that encourage you to be the person you indeed are.

The high-powered drive is intrinsic and linked to your purpose and passions. That is why it is necessary to take time out and work on these areas if you are serious about improving your drive in life. One way to look at this is to question your ambition in life to succeed. It is vital to daydream about those ideas you believe are out of reach. See yourself doing these things and imagine and hear what you may say. Focus on the positive feeling it gives you and use this energy to motivate you into action. If you do not know how to, then find someone who does and form a relationship with them. People are only too happy to help others improve their lives.

Let me tell you a story...

When I was a young woman, I experienced civil war in Nigeria. This type of trauma could have easily thwarted my drive in life. It was a time of great fear, uncertainty and sacrifice. During this time, I had to put my life on hold and become the breadwinner for my family.

Consequently, I could no longer focus on my studies, which would have enabled me to move forward with my dream of becoming a teacher. However, my focus switched to self–preservation, so my drive took a new direction. As humans, we are built to survive, and as I endured the engulfing civil war, my focus was on keeping my family safe.

It is essential to know that your drive is always within you, and the secret is to find a purpose that will keep it alive. My experiences in life have shown me that three ingredients fuel your drive: determination, willpower, and stamina. Like a long-distance runner who needs to build energy and strength to maintain concentration, speed and endurance, you too are in the race of your life, so these elements are necessary to keep you going, no matter what challenges or obstacles you face.

Determination

"Determination is the wake-up call to the human will."
Tony Robbins
American author, speaker and philanthropist

I am sure there have been times in your life when you have said "I am determined to…" Complete the blank and ask yourself, "How does that feel?"

The idea is to be aware that if you can find the evidence in your life of a time when you were determined, took action and succeeded, then this is a habit-forming behaviour you choose. It's all about how you think about the task ahead. Remember we talked about fear? Ask yourself, "Is the fear irrational or rational?" Once you have the answer to both of these questions, it is more about decision-making. Do you choose to give in to the fear and stay stuck, or do you realise that it is about your mindset and understand that failure is part of your success? Once you accept that failure is part of success, it becomes easier to take on challenges because that is how you grow and succeed.

Let me tell you a story...

Here is a Scottish legend first published by Sir Walter Scott in *Tales of a Grandfather* in 1828, more than 500 years after the Battle of Bannockburn.

The legend of Robert the Bruce and the spider is world-famous.

In the early days of Robert the Bruce's reign, he was defeated by the English and driven into exile. He was on the run, a hunted man. He sought refuge in a small dark cave and sat watching a little spider trying to make a web.

Time and time again, the spider would fall and then climb slowly back up to try.

Finally, as Robert the Bruce watched, the spider managed to stick a strand of silk to the cave wall and began to weave a web on the seventh attempt. Inspired by the spider, Robert the Bruce defeated the English at the Battle of Bannockburn.

IF AT FIRST YOU DON'T SUCCEED –TRY, TRY AGAIN!

Storytelling is a great way to learn and understand abstract and complex human traits. The story of Robert the Bruce and the spider exemplifies what you can achieve with determination. You can remind yourself of this story when you feel like giving up.

Do you want more evidence?

"Don't give up no matter what,
Eagerness is the key,
Turning on your hopes and dreams is negativity.
Everlasting joyfulness,
Running, gathering speed,
Moaning is never the answer, even if you're in need.
In times of difficulty,
Not times of sheer delight,
And if you're shocked, an excellent thing to do
is not jump up in fright.

<u>T</u>rying your best is the right thing,
<u>I</u>n all this talk about wrong,
<u>O</u>n the subject of correction,
<u>N</u>ever give up. Stay strong."

Aunty Kate

It's your turn...

It's time to get creative. You can make up your own acrostic poem for DETERMINATION as a personal reminder to keep going no matter what.

Now that you have determination under your belt, consider what willpower is and how it differs from determination. Do not confuse determination with stubbornness; determination is fuelled with a positive attitude, whereas stubbornness is fuelled with resistance.

Willpower

The dictionary definition of willpower is:

> *the ability to control yourself: strong determination that allows you to do something difficult (such as to lose weight or quit smoking)*

Willpower is **beyond** determination. You can think of it as determination on steroids! Willpower connects to your purpose, and no matter what gets in your way, nothing stops you from succeeding. Willpower is your drive.

According to most psychological scientists, willpower is the ability to delay gratification and resist short-term temptations to meet long-term goals. It is the capacity to override an unwanted thought, feeling or impulse. Procrastination and distraction are two of the nemesis of long-term gratification. They will tempt you to give up that long-term goal of perhaps saving for a holiday, a deposit for a car, or a house deposit. You may feel that going without other pleasures is not worth the effort, whereas if you include small wins and celebrations along the way, this will enable you to maintain your drive, determination and willpower to succeed.

Many people have overcome significant odds by sheer willpower. When challenges are formidable, willpower is vital. You can surf the web and find many stories of celebrities and others who have turned their lives around.

Oscar winner Halle Berry lived in a homeless shelter in her twenties when she and her mother moved to Chicago. Samuel L. Jackson, Sir Elton John and Angelina Jolie have all battled with drug and alcohol addiction and have used their willpower to stay clean for more than three decades. This attitude is the epitome of the human spirit and its willpower to not simply survive, but to thrive. Many people turn their lives around and make it part of their purpose to help others in a similar situation. Transformational stories inspire you to make changes and find the help you may need when facing your demons.

Domestic violence and abuse leave many women feeling worthless, devastated and useless. Coming out of such darkness needs absolute willpower to rebuild a life. Once these women find the courage to take action, they soon realise that at all times, they have the will and drive to create the change they need to escape their detrimental situation. Fear and the idea that they are a saviour keep them prisoners to the circumstances they find themselves in. Often, when children are involved, it can exacerbate the situation, rendering the woman powerless and helpless.

Let me tell you a story...

When I found myself a young widow, I could have created a very dark hole to live in, as the youngest of my four children was only 18 months old. How on earth was I going to manage everything by myself? The mountain ahead appeared way too high and difficult to climb.

Although I was aware of my determination because it had previously supported my goals, this situation was beyond what I had ever experienced. I had to dig deep. During this effort, I realised there was more help I would need to move beyond my trauma. I connected within and relied on my positive mindset to reveal strong willpower that enabled me to take back control of my life. I could not change what happened, but I could choose to find a new path for my children and myself.

I decided to put the children at the centre of my recovery. Everything I did was to protect, nurture and care for my children's well-being. It was a time of change, and I knew I needed to ask for and accept help from others. It was time to lean on my friends who would support me to move forward with my goals. I also had to make new friends outside of my profession as a midwife. I developed good relationships with the mothers of my children's friends who would help me with childcare. During this time, I ignited the drive to become more community orientated. This decision stirred a new passion within me that would allow me to travel a new path.

"Follow your passion, be prepared to work hard and sacrifice, and above all, don't let anyone or anything limit your dreams."

Donovan Bailey,
Olympic Gold medallist

Stamina

With stamina, you can sustain physical or mental exertion for long periods. Stamina is the strength and energy you need to maintain working towards a goal, a marathon or building a business. Increasing your stamina enables you to endure discomfort or stress when carrying out an activity. As you build stamina, it lessens fatigue and exhaustion. High levels of stamina permit you to perform your daily activities at an increased level while using less energy.

Willpower and determination are not enough without stamina, and stamina is the fuel that allows you to carry out your goal, boosted by steely willpower and steadfast determination. When you put all of these three elements together, nothing can stop you from achieving success, whatever that is for you.

After many years of working towards numerous goals, I have increased my stamina. It is always reassuring when you have this understanding of yourself reflected at you by others.

One weekend, I had several things to do. On the Saturday, I distributed leaflets for two hours as part of my political work. After that, I went home to make and eat lunch. Later that afternoon, I drove one and a half hours across London to visit a friend who had been recently bereaved. It was not until around midnight that I left to navigate the 30 miles back home.

The following day, I arose and went for my usual 10,000 steps walk. I went to church to support a friend who had a one-year memorial service for her late husband at midday. After the service, I went to her house for lunch. Next, I drove a short distance to join a community street party as part of their month-long activities to improve community engagement. I was there until 8 pm.

I talked and danced with a friend during the street party when she remarked, "How do you do all of those different activities each day? You have great stamina." This statement may not seem strange, but it is considered remarkable when you think I am over 70 years young.

The above description is not unusual for me, but since we are coming out of lockdown, where I was housebound for 18 months, it is refreshing to realise that my old stamina had not left me; it simply needed rekindling!

Olympians are prime examples of humans who take stamina and endurance to the limit. It is not just the marathon runner who needs to build stamina, but also the sprinters, gymnasts and high jumpers who rely on their stamina to maintain the high levels of energy to reach world records. I acknowledge that we are not all Olympians, but the same concept of practice, repetition and keeping active builds stamina, thus creating the desired results for each person.

It is important to note that we have just witnessed another great Olympics in Tokyo whilst writing this book. I am bringing this to your attention because these great men and women have experienced the limiting impact of Covid-19 in the last 18 months (March 2020 – August 2021) of their preparation. Yet, they still managed to win gold medals and break world records. How? Because they had been building their stamina for years, and when they had the opportunity to get back into training, their muscle memory and resilience played a crucial role in their speedy success back to high levels of stamina.

As we discuss stamina, let us see how you can build a life with strength.

First of all, you must keep **active**. Being active keeps your body in motion; the more you do, the more energy you build up over time. When you sit around the house and are inactive, you feel more lethargic. The answer is to spend energy to create more power over time.

Incorporate **exercise** into your day. You could walk in nature, swim or find out what you love to do that gives you a buzz. It could be dancing, gardening or cycling. I enjoy swimming, walking and dancing, and these have become my non-negotiables, so I have to do one of these activities daily.

Find time to be still and **meditate**. It is essential to engage in 'active rest' to empty your mind and be still, which is the art of being. You could also consider Pilates or yoga as it focuses the mind through breath work.

Everyone has a tune that makes their feet tap or chill out. It has been proven in many studies that **music** feeds the soul and can lower heart rate, improve mental agility and increase endorphins.

Lastly, there is no substitute for gaining energy than through **healthy eating**. A healthy life needs to include slow-release energy-providing foods in your daily diet. Some of the foods I regularly eat include bananas, salmon, eggs, avocado and leafy greens, which help me sustain my stamina. You can find many exciting and delicious ways to prepare and cook healthy foods to enjoy them. As our bodies are approximately 60-70% water, you must regularly replenish your water level throughout the day to maintain hydration for energy and concentration and high stamina levels.

As you journey through this book, you will realise that it is not one thing that allows you to enjoy your life with a sense of purpose, fulfilment and happiness. It takes many traits that you need to consciously desire and become the person you need to be to achieve everything you want from life. So far, we have revealed it takes:

Purpose	Drive
Determination	Mindset
Willpower	Faith
Stamina	Motivation

*"You cannot be determined if there is no willpower
to achieve the goal-driven by purpose."*

Aunty Kate

Aunty Kate's Learning Points...

◊ Ensure you keep your energy high by doing what you love. You cannot drive on an empty fuel tank.

◊ Set meaningful goals that will fuel your motivation to achieve them.

◊ Foster intrinsic motivation so that you are in control of your success through making positive choices.

◊ Accept failure as part of the success.

◊ Do not confuse determination with stubbornness. Determination is fuelled with a positive attitude, whereas stubbornness is fuelled with resistance.

◊ Use universal evidence, stories and metaphors to boost your drive.

◊ Willpower is your unstoppability power to achieve your goals with steeling determination and drive.

◊ Stamina is the strength and energy you need to maintain working towards a goal, a marathon or building a business. Boost yours daily.

One last thing...

When you find the one thing you are passionate about, your drive, determination and willpower to succeed are fuelled. You become unstoppable. Being connected to your purpose, defining your mission and setting goals intensifies these traits on which you can develop the stamina to keep you going, no matter what challenges you face. As humans, it's a challenging yet satisfying habit to view failure as part of the road to success. Sustain your drive with evidence, stories and metaphors to consolidate your I CAN mindset. Remember to create daily habits such as keeping active, eating healthily and meditating to maintain a high stamina level.

Chapter Six:
Building Resilience

Assertiveness, Finding Your Voice, Conviction in Yourself

"Resilience is knowing that you are the only one that has the power and the responsibility to pick yourself up."

Mary Holloway
Resilience coach and founder of ResilienceCafe.com

When I talk to people experiencing loss, challenges and difficulties, I ask them a straightforward question that helped me during my loss. "How are you coping?" Many people find it challenging to ask a question like this to someone who has just experienced a death in the family. Not addressing the elephant in the room was my experience after the deaths of my baby and husband.

This question opens a floodgate for women to express how they feel at that moment. Many women who know or have heard about me, respond with a question rather than an answer. "Oh, I do not know how you did it?!" 'It' refers to my story and how I coped and bounced back from my experiences of loss and challenge. Sometimes they will comment, "I don't feel like going out anymore" or "I am relying on my friends to help me through" or "I'm struggling with the kids as I have to do everything myself." Their responses all depend upon what challenges they are coping with, especially who they have 'lost'. The common thread all these women have is the notion of getting themselves together and bouncing back to a new everyday life.

After listening to their words, I find it comforts them if I share a similar personal story that reflects empathy, compassion and understanding of what they are also going through in their lives. Taking this path provides further opportunities to offload their challenges to experience a sense of relief.

We all experience profound dark moments during our lifetime, whether it is the loss of a loved one, a marriage break-up or financial challenges; you can often feel like it's the end.

You might ask yourself, "How am I ever going to laugh again? Get back up and enjoy life or make new friends who will accept me, baggage and all." When creating new friends, you must be mindful of letting new people into your circle because you are vulnerable and need to be careful that no one takes advantage of you. The answer is to look for the chink of light in the darkness. It may be sparked by a thought, what someone says to you, or a feeling that you need to do something about it for yourself. You know you need to create change. You know you need to feel better. You know you need to get back up again; the question is… HOW?

Resilience is at work when you find that power within is ready to rise again after you experience difficulty. Resilience is finding the divine spirit within and trusting that you have what it takes to dust yourself down and get back up again. Resilience is the essence of our humanity, bestowed on us by a heavenly power that enables us to carry on, regardless of trauma, earthquakes and terror attacks.

Resilience Theory argues that it's not the nature of adversity that is most important, but how we deal with it. There are numerous ways to define resilience, including the following:

"…the ability to bounce back from adversity, frustration and misfortune…"

Janet Ledesma
Professor of Department of Leadership
Andrews University, Michigan

Let me tell you a story that exemplifies bouncing back from adversity…

Losing my baby was very traumatic. You wake up to feed your baby, but there is no baby to feed.

When you have a baby, joy is the overwhelming emotion, and suddenly that joy is taken from you. When told you no longer have a baby, what are you to do?

It was such a blessing that my culture helped me because of how they look at life when you experience the loss of a loved one. They say, "Life follows death." They believe it is the will of God, and you cannot question him but learn to accept what happens as a way of learning and strengthening your spirit and faith. Strong faith enables you to cope with life and loss.

My mum said, "That life, when taken from you, suggests there is another life to come." Mother knows best, and you trust her with deep respect. She shared her wisdom by saying, "The baby does not belong to you; it's a child of God and was on a short mission." She believed that the baby's mission was to challenge and strengthen my faith in God.

I had taken a picture of the moments just after the baby's birth when he was still alive. Although I was pleased to have had the opportunity to take that picture of my son and use it as a memory of his life, my mother told me to destroy it as that baby did not belong to me, and he had returned to God. Keeping it is a powerful reminder of the loss and does not help move forward.

My mission is to help you learn from your experiences and from mine and other remarkable people who have been in the depths of despair, yet managed to rise and live a fulfilled and happy life. Along with my own stories, I often share the experiences of others who have shared with me, keeping them anonymous. These are harrowing stories of real people finding solutions that allowed them to bounce back.

If you are in this situation right now, I urge you to look in your community for solace and answers that will strengthen you as you begin to rise from your darkest hour. Community and church groups are one source of comfort and understanding, and you must never underestimate their power in restoring your faith, optimism and hope for the future. Another source of leaving the pain and hurt behind you is volunteering. When you focus on helping others, it can help take your mind off your problems. It is also a way of making new friends and building relationships with like-minded people who can support you on your journey of building a new life.

After losing my baby, I found it comforting to help and support other mothers who had the same experience. Being a midwife increased my levels of influence as the mothers had never thought that a midwife would lose a baby. Armed with this knowledge, these women immediately trusted me and increased their confidence in my suggestions to help them overcome their grief. Having empathy was a powerful support in allowing me to move forward. Because I had been through the same things, they felt comfortable sharing their deepest thoughts about their loss.

It is vital to mention that when you lose someone you love, it takes great courage to dig deep and find the resilience to get back up again. We must celebrate this influential human trait and not trivialise it as another day-to-day task, taking it for granted. It is like a muscle that needs flexing and training. The more you choose to use it, the stronger you become and the less likely you will remain down for long when faced with life's challenges.

Assertiveness

Resilience is a beautiful thing. Not only do you get to practice and strengthen your bounce-back skills, but it also provides a gift so you can move forward with confidence. Often in life, especially if you are a people-pleaser, it can be challenging to ask for what you want or, even more importantly, to set boundaries to protect yourself. It's like putting on a wetsuit when you want to swim in calmer waters, and the wetsuit offers an additional layer of protection. Assertiveness is a skill that is not always taught or quickly learned.

What does it mean to be assertive? Before looking at what it means, you should consider what it does **not** mean, as assertiveness sometimes is misconstrued. Assertiveness is not being pushy, forceful or demanding; instead, it is confident, sure and decisive.

When you are assertive, it allows you to feel in control, set personal and professional boundaries, and gain confidence that what you say comes from a place of love, respect and dignity. One of the misinterpretations of assertiveness is the other person's perception, mood and timing.

Like many other skills, assertiveness needs practising. I implore you to learn some assertiveness skills. Here are a few tips to help you:

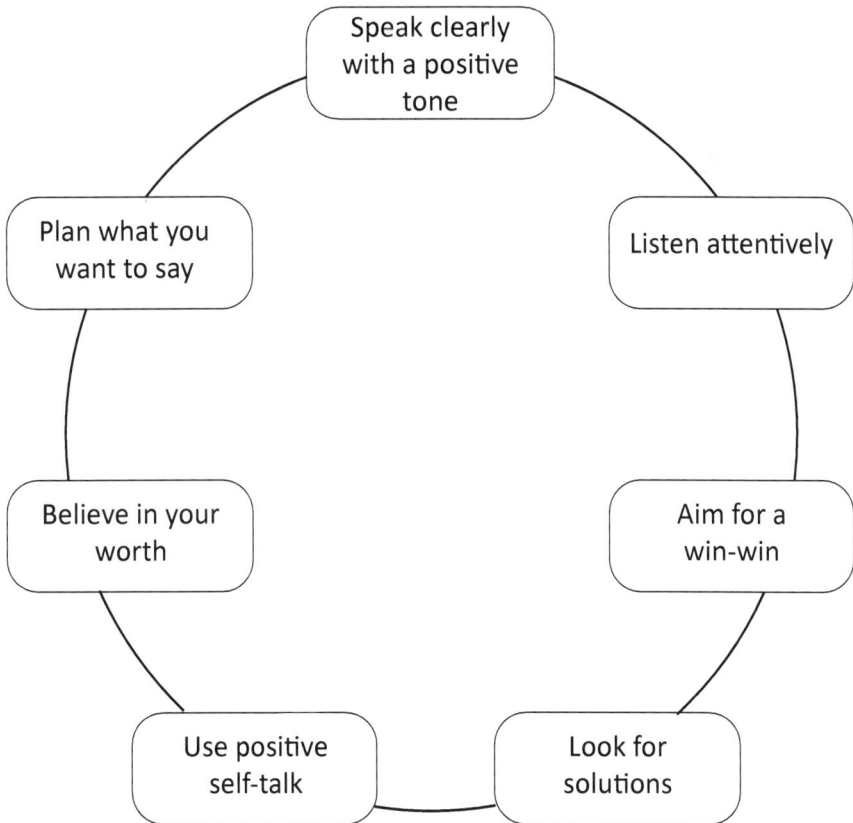

Speak clearly with a positive tone

Plan what you want to say

Listen attentively

Believe in your worth

Aim for a win-win

Use positive self-talk

Look for solutions

There is more to being assertive than the words you use. Tonality in your voice can also mean the difference between well-received words or the person taking offence. You should also consider your body language. You can always tell what someone means when their words, facial expressions and body language do not say the same thing. It is at a subconscious level that your body operates.

Let's consider this concept using the everyday phrase 'two-faced', when you say something to someone and you know you do not mean it. There will always be a clue in your body language. It's like receiving a gift that you do not like; your face and posture tell the person what you think of it. Another time that your body tells the truth is when you are trying to be brave when getting a job, finding a scurrying mouse in the house, or getting in a car for the first time when learning to drive.

Here are three ways you can use body language to be assertive.

1. Good eye contact
2. Congruence with your facial expressions
3. Upright posture

As stress bites, it becomes increasingly difficult to achieve a balance between different demands. We take on more and more but feel less and less able to cope. We become overloaded and overwhelmed, and this undermines our resilience.

Assertiveness helps us to communicate our needs. It allows us to say no to new demands, put ourselves first and gain better balance. Doing so allows us recovery time and builds our ability to bounce back stronger.

As the author of the book *Assert Yourself*, Gael Lindenfield reminds us, however, being assertive does not guarantee our needs will be met, but opens up the possibility of negotiation. And this is the route to setting new, more reasonable boundaries.

There are many incidences where I had to develop assertiveness to establish and create boundaries that allowed me to look after my children as a widow, whilst still focusing on myself and my work as a midwife. Creating boundaries and developing my assertiveness became increasingly important as the children grew. I began to work within the community and was promoted as a midwifery sister within my field of expertise. Juggling many roles required those two disciplines.

I believe that developing the skill of assertiveness is a must if you are ambitious like me and are on a mission to make a difference, especially within your community. I had to learn how to make myself clear and understood without giving anyone an opportunity to misunderstand my communication. Being clear in your communication is a must when you assert yourself to protect yourself.

You need to work on time management to be efficient and effective in whatever you choose to do for leisure or work. I am a very accommodating person, but it became too much sometimes when people used to ask me to do something at a time that was not convenient for me. At first, I used to say yes, but I soon realised that I was suffering at other people's expense. Whilst I wanted to help them, there needed to be a balance. Once I understood this, I was able to make the necessary changes and learn how to say no assertively, and without guilt.

I remember one women's conference where the organiser knew me and knew that I have a reputation for being flexible. However, without confirming with me, she included me in the event without even bringing it to my attention! But with so little notice, I had to find the courage to be assertive and tell her no, that it was too late and that she had not given me enough time to organise my diary. One of the significant lessons you have to learn is to be assertive without guilt. I still felt guilty at this time in my life, even though she had taken liberties with my time. One way to overcome guilt when you say no is to be aware of your boundaries; then, when you have to say no, you respond with grace, gratitude and ease.

As I am writing this chapter, a divine interruption occurred. I was dealing with an insurance claim regarding a leak in my kitchen. I thought I would share this little story because it meant I had to be assertive with the insurance company.

The HomeServe insurance company wanted to fix the problem, but they told me I had to get onto my home insurance as the kitchen units needed moving. Of course, this felt like an inconvenience, but I understood and contacted my home insurance. Before I knew it, there was a game of ping-pong going on with the two insurance companies. I decided, STOP! I knew this was a time to be assertive and tell them what I was expecting as a customer who paid my premiums promptly. The critical and urgent matter was to stop the leak from causing any further damage due to dampness and flooding.

I decided to email the companies with my repair expectations so that I would not be piggy in the middle of their political games. When you know your boundaries, rights and flexibility level, you can stand in your power and calmly be assertive. When were you last assertive?

Finding your voice

Glossophobia is the fear of public speaking, and many people fear public speaking more than death. Lisa Fritscher's online article in https://www.verywellmind.com/glossophobia-2671860 states that some experts estimate that as much as 77% of the population has some anxiety regarding public speaking.

It does not have to be public speaking that stops women from speaking out; it is often something simpler. Some women find it difficult to speak up in their families for fear of rejection, criticism and belittlement. You can even go back into childhood, and you will find an event in your past that has manifested the fear of speaking out, never mind the fear of speaking in public.

Culture, upbringing and environment all play a significant part in your development of self-esteem, self-worth and confidence. If anyone impedes this development, women find it exceptionally challenging to speak out or speak up.

Many African cultures and religions are patriarchal; therefore, women are suppressed in many ways and still viewed as second-class citizens, only good enough to bear children and chained to the kitchen sink. Many groups of women and individuals in some African and Asian countries have found their voice to support better education for girls. Malala Yousafzai, who at the age of 17 in 2014 won the Nobel Peace Prize, was shot in the head by the Taliban as a young girl for daring to go to school. She used the experience to find her courage and speak out even more in favour of education for girls. She says:

> ### *"When the whole world is silent,*
> ### *even one voice becomes powerful."*

Africa's first female Head of State, Ellen Johnson Sirleaf, known as the 'Iron Lady', is no stranger to speaking out about the things she believes in. Speaking directly to women and girls, she says:

*"To girls and women everywhere, I issue a simple invitation.
My sisters, my daughters, my friends; find your voice."*

Before I found my voice, I attended many conferences. I felt inspired yet scared when I watched these amazing women stand and talk passionately about themselves and women's issues. I believed I could never do such a thing. There was such a battle raging inside me because I knew I could add to what they said to help many women and girls. I had all of this experience and expertise, yet I could not bring myself to be one of those women who stood on stage.

The conferences always had one thing in common; the topic of education for girls was always high on the agenda. Whenever these words echoed in my head, they always brought me back to the person who inspired me most. Inside of me was a story longing to be told about a unique African man who believed in gender equality. This man had encouraged me to find my voice and speak my truth for the benefit of others. He filled me with the belief that education provided a stable future, expanded your understanding of the wider world and was your ticket out of poverty, deprivation and marginalisation of women. This man was my loving father.

He, too, could be described as being marginalised by his fellow countrymen as they continued to question his stance on education for girls. He did not care about what they thought or said, especially when they reminded him that he had five sons who should be highly educated. They dared to question whether he would have enough money to send them to school as well as his only daughter. Instead, he focused on ensuring that his daughter would not face the same constricting fate as many other girls who married young and have babies, chaining them to a life of domesticity. He wanted his daughter to experience the fullness of education to reach her true potential. My father's dream was for me to become a nursing sister of the highest calibre. He believed in taking every chance to make the most of education so that you could be the best person possible and be beneficial to your community and family.

Yet here I was, a grown woman and still hesitant about sharing my story. Perhaps this had something to do with my African culture, where women are often 'seen and not heard'. After all, I came to the UK in 1971 as a young bride full of hope and excitement, and it takes many years to lose limiting beliefs as to what you have always believed to be true. Believing that women should be seen and not heard was endorsed because there were not many women of colour who stood on stage and spoke freely about themselves, their story and their purpose. Over time, I gradually decided I CAN speak on stage, so I made it my mission to attend as many conferences as possible. During this time, the familiar African gentleman's voice resounded in my head, saying, "Education is for boys and girls, so always do your best, because once you respect and value education, you create a positive cycle for your children to engage positively with education."

The irony was that nothing held me back from sharing my wisdom and story when I worked with women individually, gradually extending to small groups. In this situation, I was a confident woman who believed in herself. I began to feel it more and more every time I shared stories about my education and the losses I experienced in life, which would help my patients move forward with their lives.

After some time, I realised that these women were genuinely interested in me and my story. I remember meeting several women who had come to me personally for advice. Some of these women had an urge to become part of their children's school community by putting themselves forward as a school governor. Yet, they still could not find their voice with such a calling inside. They were looking for someone to believe in them, and that someone was me. By sharing my stories openly and honestly, they felt safe approaching me. They could see that if someone like me could learn to speak out, then with encouragement, determination and a sprinkling of self-belief, these women could find their voices and become involved in what they believed.

These conversations allowed me to reflect on the advice I was giving the women and girls I was working with at the time. The satisfaction I felt spurred me to enter the political arena, so I could make a difference in the lives of the women I worked with as a midwife. It was time to not only find my voice but to share it.

It's your turn...

What are you passionate about? Which part of YOUR story exemplifies your passion? Write a paragraph or bullet points or draw a picture that represents that significant part of your story, like I did to overcome my fear of public speaking, to share my message and make a difference. I was beginning to find a purpose that was bigger than my fear of public speaking.

I knew nothing about political parties but knew that politics could allow me to create change. I threw myself into this mission and learned about the different political parties in the UK, what they stood for, and how their policies helped change communities. After a while, I could choose with whom I wanted to align myself. As a woman of colour, I aligned myself with the party I decided would allow me to express my viewpoints and voice without prejudice. I felt blessed with the people around me who encouraged me to stand for positions such as an Ethnic Minority and Women's Officer.

Having found the courage to go after my dream once more, messages from my peers propelled me to speak out for those voiceless women. Having a purpose reinforced my steely determination to seek high positions of influence and change. Could I dare to believe that a woman of colour could put herself forward for selection as a councillor? As I was venturing outside of my comfort zone, doubts consumed all of me. I did not know all of the requirements needed to be a councillor and whether or not I could uphold such a position of trust and service. I believed that it would give me a platform to be one of those women who stood on stage that I had admired for such a long time.

Conviction

According to the Oxford English Dictionary, below are the different meanings of 'belief' and 'conviction'.

Belief: an acceptance that something exists or is true, especially one without proof.

Conviction: the quality of showing that one is firmly convinced of what one believes or says.

When does belief become conviction?

Belief is something we feel in our hearts and know in our minds to be true. However, when you talk about having conviction, it comes from a deeper place – your soul. It knows that something you believe in originates from a higher plane. It is a divinity; it is a belief in God. Whether you are faced with something extraordinary or challenged, your deep conviction knows that God has designed it that way so you can learn a lesson that will not only help you but allow you to support and help others from your experiences. Conviction is what you need to overcome any adversity you encounter with acceptance, and a knowing that all will be well in the end.

At the height of lockdown, when the world seemed to stop, one old soldier marched on. This elderly gent captured the hearts of the nation during very challenging times. His conviction came from within, and it was clear to everyone just how strong, gentle and kind his spirit was, despite his advancing years and survival of a world war. I am, of course, talking about Captain Sir Tom Moore, who decided to walk one hundred laps of his garden with his Zimmer frame, representing his one hundred years on earth. He never wavered, and his family's love supported him in achieving his set goal.

Nothing was going to get in the way of doing this task each day. His experience had taught him that he was capable of anything on which he focused his mind. The conviction of his capacity and ability to reach the finishing line was palpable. Of course, the media soon learned of his quest and followed him right to the very end. A man who set out to raise a few pounds for the NHS was astonished to realise that his brave efforts would amount to almost £33 million! Consequently, his actions also made him a celebrity, and he was knighted by Her Majesty The Queen. He was visited by his favourite singer, Michael Ball, and even experienced the Red Arrows flying by in his honour. When you live by conviction, great things happen, and you can also create extraordinary opportunities to support and empower others.

The nation's hearts were broken not long after his momentous achievement when he passed on. The entire UK and world celebrated his life with a heavy heart but knew he demonstrated genuine love and commitment to his family and others. Captain Sir Tom is an example of a man who lived his life with conviction and purpose to make a difference in the lives of others.

When I lost my husband and was left to bring up four children on my own, I believed then that the world had ended. Flying around in my head were many questions that fuelled my anxiety, heartache and hopelessness. How would I cope without any help and support for the children? How would I be able to maintain working as a midwife? My finances had diminished, and now I worried about how I would manage a home and bring up four young children with less money. I guess I was not different from other young mothers who lost their soulmates too young. But in the pain and darkness of death, initially it is difficult to see any spark of light. The only constant I had amid my despair was my Christian faith and the saying in my culture that "God does not give you a load you cannot carry". Even though I may have fleetingly thought God had abandoned me, I knew deep down that He was my saving grace. The juxtaposition of these two emotions ignited the spark I needed to find a hint of light that would guide me to a brighter and better place.

A sense of knowing and a belief that God never really abandons us was the catalyst I needed to create the deep conviction that all would be well in the end. One poem that springs to mind when we feel abandoned by God is the beautiful and encouraging words of *Footprints in the Sand*:

"My precious child,
I love you and I would never leave you.
During your times of trial and suffering,
when you see only one set of footprints,
it was then that I carried you."

Anon

Conviction is not easy to achieve except when you develop a mindset that looks to the future. It is all about having a vision and being forward-looking in thoughts, words and actions. Without action, you will remain stuck. Even the smallest of steps is better than no step at all.

"The journey of a thousand miles
begins with a single step."

Lao Tzu
Ancient Chinese philosopher and writer

The secret is not to look at the finishing line, as that will overwhelm and keep you stuck in your comfort zone. It is in being mindful of each step that enables you to make significant progress forward. It is okay to raise your head and look over your shoulder to see how far you have come. Illuminate your path with the energy you create from being connected with your vision and mission. Always make sure it is more significant than you and allows you to serve others. When you commit to living your life, conviction naturally follows with clarity and confidence for partners.

Building resilience develops and improves your assertiveness and ability to find your voice and strengthen a deep conviction within yourself. You no longer fear failure but see it as part of growing and reinforcing the divine power and gifts bestowed and sharing with others and the world. When this magical moment arrives, you know it is your **Time for Purpose**. You become fearless in pursuing your goal because you no longer see ego, but focus on the benefits you bring to others through your vision and mission. Know your purpose, know your path and illuminate it with divine energy to become the change-maker our world needs.

Strengths such as gratitude, kindness, hope and bravery are your armour and protective factors against life's adversities, helping us adapt positively and cope with physical and mental illness (See note on Fletcher & Sarkar in Appendix).

Aunty Kate's Learning Points:

◊ Learn and practise how to talk about emotionally challenging subjects such as death, divorce and failure as it builds resilience.

◊ Focus on your response to adversity and challenges rather than the event itself.

◊ Explore a story that will enable you to overcome your challenge – look to others who have walked a similar path.

◊ Find the learning in your challenges; this will fuel you to move forward.

◊ Explore a purpose from your challenges – after losing my baby; I decided to help other mothers in the same situation.

◊ Become assertive – speak your mind with compassion and truth.

◊ Find your voice – create a ripple effect by sharing your story and encouraging others to do the same.

◊ Conviction is a God-given gift that drives you forward with unstoppable power.

◊ Resilience strengthens by falling and rising many times.

One last thing...

Building resilience happens over time, and it's about learning to have a positive response to challenging situations. Know that both falling and rising strengthens your resilience, and it is okay, for it is part of your journey. Build your resilience by developing assertiveness skills, finding your voice and sharing your story despite the emotional challenges faced. When you live a life fuelled with passion and purpose, you unleash the God-given gift of conviction that will make you unstoppable in your mission.

Kate at 15

Chapter Seven:
Self-Empowerment

Join Groups, Read and Learn

I want to begin this chapter by exploring what the SELF means. Often, many women will look externally for acknowledgement, approval and acceptance. It is not their fault, but if we are to blame anyone or anything, it would be the environment we grow up in. A close second reason for women developing this limiting mindset is culture. To move forward and let go of these destructive limiting beliefs of being 'not good enough' or 'not worthy', we have to go on an inner journey to discover who we are. In principle, this may seem an easy task, but it takes great courage to look within and accept who we are, including our faults. You begin a beautiful, loving, life-changing journey when you choose to embrace all of yourself.

According to the Oxford English Dictionary, the definition of SELF is:

> *a person's essential being that distinguishes them from others, especially considered as the object of introspection or reflexive action.*

Reflecting on the above definition of SELF, what springs to mind is that we are all unique. Just as we have unique fingerprints, irises and voices, it is time to believe that your soul and personality are individual.

You learn to look outside of yourself at the world as a child. Once on this journey, it becomes disempowering as you begin to compare yourself to others, find faults according to the media and absorb family limiting beliefs into your being. As suggested in the aforementioned definition, the journey to SELF is an inner voyage of discovery, connection, and knowing.

Let's go back in time. Think of a time when you were a young, fearless and curious child. Every day was a joy and an adventure as you discovered more and more about yourself and the world you live in as you learned to walk, talk and ride a bike. Moreover, the people around you influenced and shaped your mind, behaviour and personality. You had an air of confidence borne out of encouragement from your parents. Although, I do have to mention that if your childhood was troubled, you would begin your journey on the back foot. But never fear; this is no excuse for moving forward and discovering your greatness. This inner journey will include much healing because I am sure there have been times when you have criticised yourself instead of being compassionate and kind.

> *"Above all, be true to yourself, and if you cannot put your heart in it, take yourself out of it."*
>
> **Anon**

There are many psychological and medical reports on SELF. According to a report featured on the BetterHelp website, author and life coach Dylan Buckley suggests that "a strong sense of self is vital, with so many external influences and variables that can instantly change our lives and pull the roots out from where we stand." A true sense of self enables you to go through any storm you may come across without being swayed by the winds of change. Additionally, a healthy sense of self keeps you grounded and on the right path.

A sense of self is the perception of oneself. The key is to become aware of who you genuinely are from the inside out. A sense of self also links to how you feel about yourself, your level of self-esteem and your confidence. Your accurate self-perception is critical because it lays the foundation for every other aspect of your life.

On the other hand, a strong sense of self breeds confidence and ambition, even when facing adversity. Consequently, a strong sense of self is paramount. The secret is knowing how to gain it.

Essential to developing a sense of self is adopting responsibility for your thoughts, words and actions, which impact your personal growth.

Let me tell you a story...

I learned the importance of taking responsibility as the route to personal growth and satisfaction from an early age. As the eldest of seven children, it seemed culturally innate to be responsible for my younger siblings. This perception manifested loudly during the Nigerian Civil War when I had to become a second 'mum' to my younger brothers and sister. My father had to leave the village to engage in farming deeper into the countryside, whilst my mother became the breadwinner by trading in the markets. Whilst my mother was out doing the best she could for her family, I was left to look after the daily welfare of the other children.

Although my father worked in the neighbouring countryside, he would be gone during the week to return home at the weekends with an arm full of harvest for us. It was a grand celebration having my dad at home each weekend, where we could engage in 'normal' family life. It was always sad to see him go back to work, but I understood why he did what he did for his family; he wanted to ensure that we were nourished as I grew older.

We were fortunate to have food on the table, as many other families in the village struggled to eat each day. The lack of nourishment for many children resulted in them suffering from 'kwashiorkor', a severe form of malnutrition. I also think my parents' positive attitudes and work ethic created our good fortune. They would both do whatever it took to ensure they could look after their seven children. My parents passed down this family trait to me as part of leading good lives by example.

Looking after five boisterous brothers and one sister made me mature quicker than other girls aged 15. You could say I matured overnight. Most girls my age were young people attending parties, going out, and generally having fun. I sacrificed these precious years, yet felt very happy and fulfilled. When I did find time to be with my friends, I felt exceptionally adult-like and proud that I could cope with the role of being a 'mother' to six other children at such delicate age.

During the Civil War, all schools were closed. Consequently, my duties changed, and I had to enter the world of petty trading. My mother expected me to buy then sell products to make a profit to add to the family pot, ensuring that we had enough money to continue having a balanced diet to maintain a well-nourished body. A healthy body is a healthy mind. I followed in my mother's footsteps and learned the ropes as she continued to trade in this way. Knowing I was making my mother happy filled me with great pride and a sense of purpose. I believe the one element of my success was the commitment I gave to my tasks.

As I reflect on my young adult years, all the effort I put into looking after my siblings and developing a strong sense of self was appreciated by my peers and family then and still is today. My family and community held me in high esteem for choosing to do the selfless and right thing at the time. Sometimes the sacrifices we make earlier on in our lives do not reap the benefits until the time is right, which could be decades later.

Responsibility

Awareness of self is vital to developing a sense of responsibility. First of all, you need to understand the meaning and significance of that word. The Oxford English Dictionary definition is:

"the state or fact of having a duty to deal with something or of having control over someone"

You are responsible for your thoughts, words and actions, including responses to situations and people. Many people find taking ownership of responsibility challenging, but life will be tricky until you learn to accept that you are responsible.

When you do not accept responsibility, the result is blaming, accusing and complaining about anything and everything under the sun. My experience and wisdom assure me that the path to success, fulfilment and peace is fuelled by taking responsibility for the happiness in my life.

Let me share a great metaphor that demonstrates that responsibility is your decision based on your experiences, values, beliefs and life, not other people's opinions.

Long ago, a farmer entered the great city of Norwich with his son and a donkey. The man was riding the donkey, and the son led it with a rope.

No sooner had they entered the city, they heard a voice say,

"How disgraceful! See how the man sits on the donkey, like the Lord of the Manor, while his son runs ragged."

On hearing this, the farmer jumped off the donkey and set his son on top while he walked beside it. In the next street, more attention was given to the trio. A passer-by commented,

"Look at that the boy! He plays the Young Pretender while his poor old father trudges along."

Deeply embarrassed, the boy asks his father to join him.

Turning the corner onto the next street, a woman selling bat legs and toad venom spat out, "See what has become of the human race. No sensitivity to animals. Look at the poor donkey! Its back is about to break with those two on top. Disgraceful!"

Hearing this, the boy and his father dismounted immediately and began to walk beside the donkey. After about fifty yards, a market stallholder shouted out,

"I thought I was stupid, but look at these two. What's the point of having a donkey when it doesn't do any donkey work?"

After patting the donkey on the nose, the farmer turned to his son and said,

"Whatever we do, someone disagrees with it. Perhaps it's time we made up our minds about what we believe is right."

Traditional Oriental tale

I learned responsibility at a young age. The experience of being responsible for my siblings aligned me more with young adults than my peers. One thing that helps you develop a sense of responsibility is thinking of others, the bigger picture and a desire to be the best version of yourself. Deep within me, I have been blessed with this gift. However, it is possible to nurture and develop it at any point in your life. All it takes is knowing your values and aligning them to your decisions. Many people create difficulty by thinking that success is complex. In fact, you need to develop a positive growth mindset, become reflective and use emotional intelligence to realise that making decisions can be easy. The focus needs to be on the desired result and its feel-good factor.

It's your turn...

Think of a time when you had to take responsibility for something or someone. Why did you make that decision? What was it within you that felt like you had no option but to graciously carry out the duty or task with a positive mind and a happy heart? Your attitude is the significant difference between responding with grace and reacting with defiance to the same situations and people.

Draw a vertical line down the middle of a piece of paper or notebook. On the left-hand side, write down a list of things you like to do without complaining. Write down things you have to do but don't want to do and complain about in the other column.

Now ask yourself WHY you like to do these things without complaint, and then ask yourself the same question about WHY you don't like doing the things listed and complain about them.

This play activity begins an inner journey. You have to know why you do and don't do things or behave differently depending upon the situation and people involved. Once you become consciously aware, you can begin to make changes. When you fill your being with negativity, it stops you from being happy. With awareness comes power, because you can make different choices for your happiness and success. Shifting to a more growth mindset that is open, positive and accepting will help you become a better person than you were the day before, moving you forward in taking responsibility for your actions and outcomes.

It is easy to take responsibility when you work on your mindset, know your values and have a positive self-image. Your attitude to simple everyday living such as keeping a tidy house, cleaning your teeth and doing things to the best of your ability, is evident in how you do them.

However, there are many things that people do not take responsibility for, such as managing money, setting boundaries for their children and making the right decisions.

When you make decisions not aligned with your values, you feel negative emotions. In this detrimental state, life becomes challenging and accepting and taking responsibility creates difficulties in making those positive decisions. You enter into a cycle of blame, judgement and guilt. You are heading into a downward spiral, and nothing changes until you make a change. Furthermore, creating change needs action. Let's consider action in terms of empowerment.

Empowerment

You can be empowered in two ways. You can rely on external empowerment, or you can be in control of your empowerment or self-empowerment.

Empowerment is an external authority given to you, enabling personal power in a range of aspects such as:

◊   making decisions within your job;

◊   receiving recognition and awards to promote your standing in your field;

◊   within politics, when the community empowers you to represent them when they vote for you in an election.

External empowerment is only one way to achieve a goal, but there is still a lack of complete control. You continue to rely on others, and you are limited to what you can do and achieve. Whilst empowerment is excellent, it is not the most powerful way to make the progress you may desire for yourself. The point here is that you need to learn about self-empowerment if you genuinely want to change your life and consciously be in control of your destiny.

Personal Empowerment

It takes courage to accept responsibility for your choices, decisions and outcomes. When you are ready to create the significant change within you, you will take control of the path that will lead you to your desired success. Most people are afraid of taking control because they may fear making mistakes. It is not until you learn that failures are very much part of the success that you begin to embrace and accept them as opportunities for learning. To accept this as truth is why I say it takes courage. Courage is what is needed to make any change in your life.

After you find your courage, you are ready to control what happens to you in your life. Leading a good life is subjective to each of you, and what is suitable for one person may not be good for another. Being unique is why personal empowerment is different for each individual.

Consider a time in your life when you felt powerless, in situations such as being in a toxic relationship, or your job did not satisfy you, or you lived in accommodation that you disliked. These circumstances are pretty extreme, but learning about developing your personal power can enable you to make simple choices. To make simple choices, you need to give yourself no more than two alternatives: either this or that. You can take control over when you do something. You do not have to abide by other people's rules and regulations. Self-empowerment is fuelled by being proactive. You are doing tasks and jobs before being asked. In that way, you are taking control of the situation and not responding to another person's requests.

For example, if you lose your job, you may unconsciously become passive in your job search and sit about waiting for a recruiter to find you on LinkedIn, or you could be proactive towards finding a new and better job. Proactive people will contact former colleagues, research job opportunities, update their CVs with marketable skills, and improve their networking. Some people will seek further training to enhance their skill set or participate in new activities to enhance or uplevel their existing knowledge and skill set. Self-empowerment allows you to recognise you have the power to make choices that can help you achieve your goals, dreams and vision.

Consider a situation where you sit back passively, waiting for someone else to take control. Now shift the lens and look at it through a new set of proactive eyes. What choices can you make that will enable you to regain control and make decisions that will leave you feeling positive and moving towards your goals?

Let me tell you a story...

As we entered a new millennium, it was an optimum time for a change. What would I challenge myself to achieve in this new century, this new beginning?

Watching the Remembrance Day Parade and seeing all of the officials and dignitaries parading towards the Cenotaph, I felt a sense of fulfilment for the mayor as I admired his official regalia. The bright red velvet cloak trimmed with a fur colour caught my eye. The November sunshine glinted on his golden chain of office, and I felt the power of its symbolism rush through my veins. I was impressed by what the robe and chain symbolised, and within me, I felt a strong desire to become mayor. Being a mayor represents service to your community, and I knew this was part of the bigger picture for my life; it is my purpose. The role of the mayor is strictly non-political and representative of every section of the community, mainly focused on cultivating the positive image of the borough and enhancing the well-being of its citizens.

I knew what my new goal would be, and I decided then and there that I wanted to become a mayor. That was a challenge because I did not even know where to begin, but when you consider how a black middle-aged woman becomes the Mayor of a London Borough like Enfield, you double the challenge!

The first place I started was considering what I had already achieved in my life. After all, I was engaged in local politics; indeed, this would be an excellent place to start. I asked myself, who do I know who could help me? Where should I begin looking? What qualifications and experience does one need to become a mayor? By asking myself questions, I was taking control of what my next step would

DR KATE ANOLUE – Time For Purpose

be. I became proactive in discovering all the answers I needed to help me achieve my dream.

There are several considerations to think about before becoming a mayor. Local community knowledge has to be gained by becoming a councillor first and working on behalf of the people. This local community position demonstrates intention, commitment and purpose. When you find out one answer, it always poses a new question. So being proactive is necessary to find out all of the answers and join the dots so you can create a plan that will allow you to achieve your goal.

During my quest, I discovered that the political party I belonged to were not in administration; therefore, that was an obstacle I had to overcome. First of all, I had to become a councillor of the party in administration before I could even begin the journey of becoming mayor. One of the aspects of self-empowerment is the roadblocks you endure, the dead ends you face and the disappointment encountered. But the trait of determination, having a big why and knowing that failure and mistakes were part of the road to success, empowers you to keep going with consistent action because you eventually reach your desired destination.

It took me two years to become a councillor and another 10 years to fulfil my dream of becoming mayor. So, my message to you is never to give up! You do not know how long your journey will take, perhaps a year or three or more, but you learn to enjoy every step when the goal is aligned with your purpose, passion and drive to serve others. Finding your purpose is the secret to being successful in your life, and it takes time, effort and perseverance.

I want to share some tips that will help you achieve personal empowerment.

Striving to attain personal empowerment requires focusing on your drive and identifying what you can control. You must keep an objective, goal-oriented mindset. Here are the eight tips I use to foster my power.

- **Develop a Positive Attitude**

  People who believe they control their destiny — rather than giving in to external concepts such as fate, luck, or circumstance — are more likely to take charge of their future. Cultivate a positive attitude and outlook by evaluating your strengths and weaknesses, pursuing your passions and trusting your ability.

- **Set SMART Goals**

  Measurable, achievable goals are an essential component of self-empowerment, and understanding how to set them can help you feel good about your achievements. If you want to run a marathon, start with a smaller race, increasing distances rather than trying to run 26.2 miles on day one.

- **Surround Yourself with Positive People**

  Laughter is contagious — and so are pessimism and negativity. Surrounding yourself with like-minded, motivated people can help you feel empowered to achieve your goals. Schedule time with positive friends, peers and family members if your self-esteem takes a blow. Experiencing their positivity can improve your mental well-being, minimise your negativity, and empower you to follow your dreams.

- **Take Care of Yourself First**

  Self-care includes any activity you do to feel happy and healthy. It can have everything from eating the right food and exercising, to treating yourself to a spa treatment. Scheduling time to relax and rejuvenate will make you more productive. Additionally, being kind to yourself can help you be confident in your ability to address and overcome hardship.

- **Use Positive Self-Talk**

  To live a self-empowered life, focus on what you can do instead of what you can't. For example, if you want to apply for a promotion that requires fluency in Spanish, instead of saying "I don't speak Spanish," try "I don't speak Spanish yet, and I can learn." Practising self-affirmations and displaying confidence in your ability to achieve your goals can help you take steps to achieve them.

- **Be Assertive**

  People who strive toward personal empowerment must be comfortable expressing their thoughts, ideas and needs. If you're invited to a party but have an introductory presentation the following day, let the host know you'll be leaving early to prepare. Or, if you and a co-worker are collaborating on a project, but you're doing most of the work, don't feel guilty about addressing the situation head-on and asking them to do their share.

- **Create an Action List**

  Empowered people take action, exhibit a growth mindset, and are comfortable learning and developing their abilities. They also understand that success does not come overnight but is a culmination of decisions and actions. If your goal is to finish your college degree within four years, list the activities you'll need to take to achieve that goal, such as researching financial aid options, enrolling in an online program, and establishing a study schedule.

- **Live a Self-Empowered Life**

  People who consciously decide to take control of their lives are often happier, more fulfilled, and more satisfied in their careers – taking steps to live a life that you design offers numerous benefits. If you are ready to take control of your life, write down the one goal you want to achieve, research what you need and see how you can begin that journey with the first step. Next – Take Action!

In this chapter, I have shared the definition, stories and importance of understanding Self, Responsibility and Empowerment. All of these elements are very personal to each one of you. Individual empowerment means that you take responsibility for yourself. Taking the first step is the most powerful one you can take, and only you can do that. It will help if you let go of negative emotions and traits such as blame, jealousy and guilt. It would be best if you deflected all distractions, outside influences and the opinions of others. You must then fill yourself with love, acceptance and gratitude.

It is the growth mindset that understands the necessity of personal empowerment. When you embrace and create good habits around personal empowerment in your life, you are taking control and fuelling the drive, determination and perseverance that ultimately leads to your success, fulfilment and peace. Remember to shut down negative self-talk and reframe it with words of encouragement, love and kindness. Once personal empowerment becomes part of who you are, you undoubtedly will know that the *Time for Purpose* has to be addressed now.

Aunty Kate's Learning Points

◊   Know yourself – practise introspection often. It will heighten your emotional intelligence.

◊   Become aware of who you genuinely are from the inside out.

◊   Do things because you want to, not because someone else wants it for you.

◊   Assume responsibility for everything in your life – a challenging yet rewarding task that takes time.

◊   Find the courage to empower yourself always. Be proactive.

◊   Explore ways such as joining groups, learning and reading that inspire you to take responsibility for your success.

◊   Consider and take action on my eight habits to foster self-empowerment.

One last thing...

Self-empowerment begins when your curiosity takes you on an inner journey. Knowing yourself inside and out is vital to your self-empowerment. Learn to do things you want, and let your choices and decisions reflect your internal moral compass. Be proactive and adopt responsibility at all times. Explore ways in which you can continue developing your self-empowerment, such as joining groups, attending workshops and events, and reading. Create good habits that will support your journey to becoming the best version of yourself – an empowered individual.

As Mayor of the Borough of Enfield

Chapter Eight: Service

Visibility - Engage in Your Community - Give

"Visibility
...and that visibility which makes us most vulnerable
is that which also is the source of our greatest strength."
Audre Lorde
American writer and civil rights activist

Visibility is *the state of being able to see or be seen*, which is challenging for many people. The American writer Audre Lorde was a self-described "black, lesbian, mother, warrior, poet." She dedicated her life and her writing to challenging and addressing injustices of racism, sexism, classism and homophobia.

Many people, once they find their purpose, walk the path of service. But how do you serve and ensure that you look after your needs, dreams and goals? Some people become confused over service; they often start as people-pleasers. Exploring what it means to be a people-pleaser reveals that one puts the needs of others before one's own due to the fear of being rejected, scorned or misunderstood. At the same time, a life of service includes looking after your own needs first. You cannot serve from an empty cup. This saying reminds us to make sure we engage in activities that please us and fill us with respect, love and kindness. Only then can one serve unconditionally with humility, honour and happiness.

Consider those people you admire who live lives of service; the Queen has reigned for 70 years without faltering. She made no excuses for not showing up and doing her duty as the monarch of the UK, even in her most challenging times. Mother Teresa gave her life to serving the poor, hungry and dying in Kolkata. She also did not use any excuse to help the people with the grace of God. Martin Luther King Jr was a great orator and serviceman to the black community in America. Again, he made no excuses to voice his truth in the fight for freedom. Even until his untimely assassination, he continued with the rhetoric, "I have a dream."

One could consider that purpose and service intertwine to serve people, animals or the planet. The secret is to find your aim in life to serve, which is the reason for our human existence. On your journey through life, your adversity, challenges and experiences are the lessons you learn from to grow as individuals. When you combine these life lessons with your passion, skills and knowledge, you are preparing to walk the path of service and purpose.

Some people, like me, realise their purpose early on in life. As discussed in earlier chapters, I knew as a young girl during the Nigerian Civil War that I was here on this earth to serve others. How did I know? Because I was put in situations ahead of my young years, I always conducted myself to the best of my ability and took great responsibility for positive outcomes. I never once wavered. Surprisingly, as a young woman, I found these challenges led me to a sense of fulfilment and happiness way beyond my peers.

It is essential to share some aspects that enable you to serve with an open heart and reach many people. After all, when you live a life of purpose, your values, vision and mission are the drivers to your success. But how do you reach those people who do not know you yet? One of the necessary aspects to respond to the critics who ask, "Who are you?", "What do you do?", "Why should we listen to you?" is to step outside of your comfort zone, find your voice, and speak up for those you serve. The answer lies in becoming visible. In today's world, it has never been easier with the help of the internet, social media and local community work.

With purpose comes your magnetic message. It is the consistency of putting yourself on social media and attending many local community events that people begin to see, hear and understand. It is also important to remember that your why or purpose is more significant than you. After all, you have a job to do during this life. Visibility is key to your success. How can you make a difference in people's lives if they do not know who you are, what you stand for, and what changes you want to complete in the world?

Your purpose is fuelled with passion and drive to share your learning, beliefs and the philosophy you have gained during your life experiences. These powerful teachings are the wisdom that those you wish to serve must hear. Life's traditions and lessons survive the test of time, and the stories passed down from generation to generation also create brilliant opportunities to grow.

Public speaking or glossophobia is one significant reason people keep themselves insignificant and hold back living a life of purpose. It is vital to continue developing a strong mindset that learns to silence negative self-talk to connect with your purpose and use your reason to smash through the fear. When you adopt a 'braveheart' attitude and approach, you will be amazed at what you can achieve. Remember, it is vital to be visible, and that does not only mean to be seen but also to be heard as you speak your truth while serving others.

One way to grow your confidence in sharing your message is to attend events with like-minded people. Networking is essential to reach as many people as possible. You can begin small by talking one-on-one with someone you connect with within the room. Starting with one-to-one connections will help you practice what you need to say so that your message is heard and understood. It will also grow your confidence in speaking about what impassions you. It is like everything else in life; and the more you do it, the easier it becomes. Before long, you will find yourself speaking comfortably in small groups about your message and mission and one day, you will find yourself talking on stage. There are always ways of developing your visibility.

You can increase your confidence by creating short videos shared across social media. As you become more comfortable, you can offer live recordings, run webinars and host online networking events. These practices increase your visibility, especially when raving fans share your content!

Another way in which you can gain more visibility is through the media. You can be a guest on a podcast and appear in magazines and interviews for TV and radio shows. Like me, I'm sure you will catch the visibility bug and know that this is an assured way of serving others and having a far-reaching connection with those you are here to help.

Engage in your community

Let me tell your story...

My experience engaging with my community began in Nigeria when I was a substitute mum to my younger siblings. The other mothers in the community did not see any difference in talking with me as a young girl mothering her brothers and sister. This situation was the foundation that ignited my passion for serving my community.

When I left Nigeria to come to the UK, my job also allowed me to serve in the community as a midwife. It was such an honour and pleasure knowing that I was making a difference in the lives of many new and young mothers who felt hopeless, confused and alone. Throughout engaging in community work, my eyes were opened to the level of domestic abuse experienced by many of these young women who were pregnant or had recently given birth. These circumstances ignited my mission to continue to work with women encountering domestic violence and somehow empower them to make the necessary changes to their lives. By talking with these women, I provided information that enabled them to find the support they required. All they wanted to find was comfort and a safe place to bring up their child in peace. Once again, I felt a great sense of fulfilment as I observed these women finding the courage, strength and determination to make the change.

When I worked in the hospital, I remember one particular young girl. I will call her Aisha. She was 18 and in an arranged marriage to a man who was double her age. Every Saturday, he would accompany her to the antenatal appointment as he did not work on that day. One particular Saturday, Aisha appeared without her husband, and when I naturally inquired about his whereabouts, she burst into tears, instead of a usual response. I found it challenging to understand what Aisha was saying through her distress. Fortunately, I was able to calm her down, and I was shocked at this young pregnant girl's story.

Aisha was living in the UK and had no family support. Her family lived in Asia. She was treated more like a slave than a wife and daughter-in-law by her husband and large extended family. They forced pregnant Aisha to cook and clean for them and she had to wait until they finished eating before she could eat any food. Adding to her plight, Aisha had no money and was emotionally, mentally, and physically abused. She felt hopeless and alone. Aisha was never unaccompanied so could not share her story until that day. Immediately after Aisha released her story, you could physically see the burden lifted from her shoulders. I asked her what she wanted us to do for her. Her reply was, "I am not going home."

In turn, I explained to her the support we could provide for victims of domestic abuse. Aisha wanted to go anywhere other than 'home'. Her sentiment was that she just wanted to hide. Thankfully, we were able to offer her a safe space. There are many more stories like Aisha's, and they are the driver for me to continue to serve in my local community. Whenever I share Aisha's story, I find myself transported back to that time and place.

As a consequence of this experience, I knew I could make a difference, so I joined Enfield's Women's Aid to offer my support. Working with victims of domestic abuse and Woman's Aid is an area of my life that I serve to this day. I am a co-founder of the International Consortium for Domestic Peace, and I can use all of my experience to support further women who fall victim to domestic abuse.

Find something you are passionate about and use it to serve your local community. Each of us has something that triggers a deep emotion and a desire to help others in the same situation. Whether domestic violence, children's welfare or animal rights, you will have something for which you will want to raise your voice. Serving disempowered women is part of my philanthropy. I also support others in the community through politics and civil service as part of being the Mayor of Enfield on two occasions.

Not everyone wants to enter public service or politics to serve in their local community. Many people join organisations of things that mean something to them, such as Neighbourhood Watch, Resident Associations or Love Your Borough activities. You could also think about what matters to you in your neighbourhood. Thinking does not get the job done, but once you have identified what matters most to you, the next step is to take action and join one of these groups. If you are so passionate about something, you could find the courage and start your cause and organisation. Like-minded people within these successful groups join together and work collaboratively. You too can research who can support your ideas and join forces when you are satisfied you have found the right people. All of this action relates to being of service. When you serve, there is a sense of fulfilment that often escapes you from other aspects of your life.

Let me share another story...

A young woman called Jasmine asked me if it was okay for her to shadow me when I was mayor. Of course, I agreed for her to do so. A short time later, as she was doing so well in supporting me, I asked her to volunteer in my organisation. Jasmine's first language was French as she was from Gabon in Africa; however, she spoke English equally well. Being a shy person, she was initially reticent to become involved with the other people we met along the way. However, over time she gained confidence, and I asked her to say a few words at the start of one of the conferences. Whilst afraid, she knew the only way to make progress was to say yes. She took to the stage and spoke well in front of the audience. Some more time passed, and I asked her to close one of the meetings. Once again, although English was not her first language, she could use it with great aplomb.

As Jasmine's confidence grew, it came to our attention that the French-speaking women in the community did not like to engage in the meetings. I encouraged Jasmine to start her discussions with these women to speak to them in French to change this perspective. This innovative idea ignited success, and not before long, more and more women attended. Consequently, Jasmine decided to form her organisation called Voice Out Woman. She was on a mission to be the voice for those women who were yet to master English. It was essential to her that their voices were heard in the community.

According to one Australian survey, 96% of volunteers believe that volunteering makes people happier in their lives. This belief is evident in further research showing that volunteers answer questions more positively if they participate in regular volunteering activities. Furthermore, on a global stage 70% of volunteer work does not involve any organisation but happens informally between people in their communities. Here in the UK, the National Council of Voluntary Organisations (NCVO) conducted a survey in 2019 that showed 20 million adults volunteered between 2018 and 2019 in a wide range of areas.

Community service relies heavily on volunteers to help create the change they want to see in their communities and the world. It is crucial to shift the lens of how you think because it is a virtuous action to be a person who gives without recompense. You can develop a humanitarian sense of giving, which will provide the bounties of the Laws of Attraction.

Giving

Some people give because they want to receive; they perceive giving with the attitude of 'what's in it for me' rather than recognising their actions as a gift of service. I want to note that receiving is necessary. Still, your spirit will provide the most satisfaction, especially in receiving criticism, opportunities and wisdom as part of your purpose.

Another issue some people face around service is that they never seem to receive any recognition for their efforts in their giving. If you think this way, it is time to shift the lens through the glasses you see the world.

I am a woman of service and believe giving is unconditional. When you share with an aligned heart and soul, I suggest that your perception changes. It is about loving what you do and doing what you love. This philosophy is the optimum place to find yourself on your life's path. Without your awareness, many people do recognise your work.

My experience has taught me that you need to let go of the ego around giving; instead, connect and lead with your heart. When you choose this way of giving, you do not necessarily rely on the words of others to drive you to keep going with your manner of serving, but on the force that comes from within. You act by intrinsic motivation related to your values, vision and mission.

Let me tell you a story...

In 2007, I was honoured with the Freedom of the Borough of Enfield. It emphasised the outstanding community service I had given to the town's people. I was shocked in a good way when I received this accolade because this was something I did out of love and to help others who benefited from my years of experience, expertise and learning. Adopting an enthusiastic approach to what you do each day will compound over time, and be assured that there will be many people who recognise your work as outstanding. The secret is to let go of needing to hear others acknowledge your work. After all, they are not asking you to do it, but you choose to do it as part of serving others and living a life of purpose. When connected to your goal, all you need to carry out your daily tasks is a smile that radiates the compassion and humanity within each of us.

You may have heard the saying, "You cannot pour from an empty cup." Let me explain how I understand what this phrase means. As women, we are the natural caregivers of our families. We give to others, which illustrates that we are usually the last to receive anything from ourselves. You are the vessel, and if you keep giving without replenishing, you become exhausted, overwhelmed and resentful. You will ask questions such as, "Why does no one treat me like I treat others?" As a woman of faith, the Bible tells us to treat others the way we want to be treated ourselves. This tenet is very true for me, but there is no guarantee that these 'others' live by my moral code and values. Once you understand and accept that we are all different, you can change how you think and feel about receiving.

Often when people compliment us, we deflect its power by undermining the giver's intention. For example, someone might say, "Oh, I love the dress you are wearing." Very quickly, we might respond with, "Oh, this old thing, I've had it for years!" Whereas the proper receiving response would be gratitude, and a simple "Thank You".

It's your turn...

Think about all the times you deflect receiving compliments, gestures and support; what do you say? What do you do? How could you better receive the words and actions of others with a spirit of gratitude?

It's time to create your Gratitude Journal! Find a beautiful notebook where for 30 days you can daily write down five to ten things for which you are grateful and/or thankful, such as:

- I am grateful for the air that I breath

- I am thankful for my family

- I am thankful for the trees that create oxygen

- I am thankful for having a roof over my head

- I am grateful for the love of my dog

Receiving is a powerful skill you can learn. You could think of it as the tide; it ebbs and flows. We live in a world of duality. The sun rises and sets, the moon waxes and wanes, and we have to learn to receive in giving. There is something in the psyche of women that makes them feel guilty, not worthy, or that it is not necessary to obtain. How wrong can we be? Life changes once you learn to receive a heart filled with generosity, grace and gratitude.

Do you believe in the Law of Attraction? It works on the principle of giving and receiving with a grateful heart. When you give thanks for what you have, the universe and God conspires to give you the divine right of abundance for thankfulness. Gratitude also creates a sense of freedom from material possessions and bestows a more profound understanding of worthiness within you. Life changes for the better when you practise living this way, especially when it aligns with your purpose.

When you give unconditionally, you influence many people who are happy to walk in your footsteps. In this way, the by-product of giving is that you make many unknown friends who will speak highly of you and share your message of encouragement, hope and self-worth. All of these unfamiliar friends often recognise your great work and recommend you for those awards that acknowledge everything you do in the name of service.

Find the evidence in others.

The great humanitarian Oprah Winfrey often talks about giving. This belief is a selfless sharing attitude that makes the world richer and better. She says,

> ***"The best gift anyone can give, I believe,***
> ***is the gift of sharing themselves."***

When Oprah received the first Bob Hope Humanitarian Award, she wanted to share the importance of being human. She stressed that we all want to be heard, loved, and find someone to laugh and cry with when we need it.

Service is about finding the courage to be visible, to engage in your community, and give all of yourself to that purpose, campaign, or the people you have chosen to serve. It does not matter who you are, whether the woman in the street, the mayor of your city or a celebrity like Oprah Winfrey, you are all capable of serving something or someone aligned with your values. You find yourself on the crucial mission to provide a sense of fulfilment and happiness and make a difference.

Knowing that we are all human and share the same hopes and dreams is enough to warrant your commitment to helping yourself by helping others. You transform yourself and create change in others, empowering them to find the courage to come out of their shell and allow them to shine and find the confidence to express themselves. Service is about finding a cause that is bigger than you and brings meaning to your life. You know it's **Time for Purpose** when you connect with this idea

Aunty Kate's Learning Points

◊   When you choose a life of service, being visible gives you an advantage.

◊   Explore your childhood because often hidden in those stories lies your purpose and service.

◊ Engage in your community. Share your gifts, for they will advantage and empower others, leaving you with a sense of fulfilment and purpose.

◊ Give freely of your time, efforts and gifts because you love to see others flourish.

◊ Remember, before you give to others, give to yourself first. You cannot pour from an empty cup.

One last thing...

Once you have found your passion and purpose, it will drive you with a compelling need to serve others. Service is the ultimate gift to others, and you may choose community service. When you help others, you must remember to ensure that you fill your own energy and loving cup first before you give anything to others. By adopting this rule, you will always give freely without guilt, resentment or judgement.

Receiving the Freedom of the Borough of Enfield

Chapter Nine: Success

Define Success - Look for Evidence - Celebrate

What is success?

The Oxford English Dictionary defines success as:

the accomplishment of an aim or purpose.

Defining success is different for everyone, and it's as unique as your fingerprint. Knowing and understanding what success looks like, sounds like and feels like is worth taking time to reflect, journal and daydream about its meaning for you.

> *"Your success and happiness lie in you."*
>
> **Helen Keller**
> **American disability rights advocate and political activist**

Considering the above words by Helen Keller, you could argue that success takes courage of going on the journey within. Most people measure success by achieving goals, such as passing exams and climbing the ladder within their career, and for some, it is all about how much money they have in the bank. However you measure success, it is vital to understand why success is essential to your development and growth.

Why is success important?

Success begins from birth. In the beginning, there is much extrinsic motivation to succeed. When a baby starts to crawl, the parent will put a favourite toy just out of reach so that the baby learns by moving forward; they can come close enough to touch the prize. However, when the parent is not around, the baby will have set down neural pathways to repeat the action, thus developing muscle memory. The infant soon learns 'to feel good', and therefore intrinsic motivation is instilled, and they will continue to practise crawling and reaching out for objects whether the parent is there or not.

Success experiences trigger your brain with a surge of dopamine, the body's pleasure chemicals, resulting in you feeling warm, happy and ready to face life's challenges. Success creates a rush that is addictive, so many people such as Sir Richard Branson, Arianna Huffington and J.K. Rowling continually set themselves ambitious goals, because success breeds more success.

Let me share a story...

Today, every author, speaker and entrepreneur has a deep desire to have their articles published in the famous online publication, *The Huffington Post*. But its founder Arianna Huffington struggled in the beginning to become a highly successful businesswoman in the twenty-first century.

The Huffington Post was not an instant hit, but she stood firm and took on board the highly negative views that spurred her to become bigger and better by overcoming the bouts of failure. The grit, determination and belief in herself sowed the seeds for her success. Evidence cements Arianna Huffington and *The Huffington Post* as one of the most successful outlets on the internet.

Success fosters feelings of joy and being recognised, admired and accomplished. The feeling of euphoria when your name is engraved on a plaque as millions cheer you on, as Serena Williams, the world champion tennis player, only knows too well, is also a great motivator to keep you going. The glory of success lies in making you feel happy because achieving happiness is the ultimate goal of our lives.

Success is also fuelled by determination, working hard, and focusing on your goals. You could argue that luck is an element of success, but I prefer to associate it with the Law of Attraction. The Law of Attraction drives athletes, such as Sir Mo Farrah, to go beyond their limits. It drives scientists, such as Thomas Edison, to spend countless hours on an experiment to create the first light bulb. It drives people, such as Elon Musk, to develop something fresh and innovative like SpaceX, Tesla, Neuralink and OpenAI.

Success drives us forward; it is a vital fuel of humanity. Success was significant to us in the past; it is significant to us now and will be significant to us all for the foreseeable future. Consider the topic of communication. Cave dwellers drew images on their cave walls; today, we communicate via platforms such as Zoom, and future communications such as augmented reality, automated translations and brain-computer interfaces will be the norm. However you look at success, communication is vital to help you understand, assimilate and collaborate to achieve better results. In other words, keep talking, no matter the medium you choose to use.

Let me tell you a story...

I learned the importance of success as a young girl when people in my Nigerian community in Nanka commented on how much I had matured. Facing a civil war is something that accelerates maturity in a young person. Petty trading ensured I contributed to my family's finances and looking after my siblings enabled me to accept responsibility at the tender age of 16.

This maturity resulted from embracing my challenges, duties and tasks with an open heart to do my best. My parents instilled integrity, humility and responsibility in me, reflected in my education and community engagement attitude. The compliments I received allowed me to swim through the overwhelm and sparked the fuel I needed to rely on myself to continue on the path to success. I knew that this behaviour was the right thing to do as life always worked out for me, despite my challenges. It was not too long before I embodied success which is evident throughout my life. I moved from Nigeria to the UK, raised four children on my own as a widow, and gracefully moved between careers in nursing, law and public service.

When I was a community midwife, I felt as if all of my dreams had come true. My work enabled me to connect with young mothers and their families. I believe this role was a privilege because I often became part of the family. The depth of understanding, knowing and trust built up over time allowed me to make a difference in the lives of many young mothers. It was not just professional satisfaction that I experienced, but from my heart I knew the humanitarian in me was being fulfilled. Humbled by my circumstances, I developed close bonds and friendships, which made it possible for me to accomplish my mission of being a servant to some of the most vulnerable women in my local and national communities.

So, what elements led to my success?

- Having a why, a reason, a goal.

- I chose the role I wanted to play; that of a midwife.

- To reach this trusted position, I spent years of dedication, commitment and determination studying to succeed.

- I was driven by both extrinsic and intrinsic motivation, sparked by my father's desire and my intention of becoming a nurse.

- I spent four and a half years training, followed by several years working in hospitals delivering babies to hone my expertise.

Ingredients for your success

- Having a clear focus is crucial to moving forward, regardless of the obstacles put in your path.

- Consider past experiences that illustrate you can do whatever you set your mind to achieve.

- Look to famous people you admire who also have a great story that demonstrates you can achieve what you desire and prioritise.

- Align yourself with the inner journey of connecting with your values, those principles that drive you and make decisions easy. If you do not choose wisely, your decisions haunt you with

feelings of guilt, shame and hurt. When you are in this dark
place, the light of success seems like climbing Mount Everest

My story reveals that this time in my life was both a joy and exposed
a shade of darkness that could have easily broken me. However,
being a single mum to four children was why I chose to pick myself
up and carry on. With the youngest of my four children only 18
months, losing my husband was enough to break any woman. I was
fortunate; my life experiences had prepared me for my darkest hour.
I had to dig deep and recall these at my most vulnerable times and
used the memories of the civil war in my younger days to fuel my
reason to continue.

When you connect with a purpose in life, it fuels your desire to
succeed. Life experiences are both yin and yang; there is light and
darkness and many shades. It is easy to carry on when joy knocks
on your door, but the true strength of a person is getting up time
and time again when adversity shows you its lessons. These dark
opportunities allow you to strengthen your resilience. Not only do
you enjoy the feel-good factor, but doors of opportunity begin to
present themselves, allowing you to continue on the path to your
ultimate goal and success.

I have learned from my many lessons that you must set aspiring goals
so you always have something to focus on that is more significant
than you. It becomes the catalyst to continue when life throws you
curve balls. Life is not a straightforward path, but is full of undulating
roads, twists and turns, and mountains to climb. Shaping a growth
mindset and positive attitude is the one aspect that will keep the
negativity at bay. You learn to look for the silver linings and hope.
You know to carry the sunshine within you and understand that
progress is inevitable when your strong intentions ignite action. So
be brave and take steps each day. Courage will transform your life.

Many people use age as an excuse to stop learning and moving
forward, but I am the epitome of a woman driven by the spirit,
and not the mind nor the hollow advice from people with good
intentions. Your belief in yourself is vital to stepping outside of your
comfort zone and seeing what the grass looks like on the other side.
Too many people live in fear, indecision and disconnection, not only
from others but also from themselves.

There is a certain power and energy when connecting within that enables you to continue your evolution on earth. I must reiterate that it is essential always to set goals and new challenges. Age is not the barrier, but your negative attitude and lack of nerve are two traits that will stop you from living on purpose.

Let me tell you another story...

At the tender age of 43, as mentioned previously I decided to enter the legal world and study law. As I entered middle age, I chose to educate myself further while holding down a full-time job as a community midwife. I made this decision because of the problems that presented themselves during my years as a midwife, so I chose to specialise in medical negligence. I had witnessed stressful situations, patient dissatisfaction and a lack of support for my peers. Enough was enough; I decided it was me who would make the difference. I was not prepared to sit around and wait for someone else. I knew using my grit and determination, I would succeed.

As a woman who always has a mission, I knew that I could make a difference if I educated myself in this troublesome area. After all, bringing a new life into the world is highly responsible, so understanding the systems that need to be in place was vital to improving the safety of staff, mother and unborn child. Part of this journey also opened the door to whet my political appetite, so I became the Royal College of Midwives' Midwife Steward. This position allowed me to access peers' support when queries, such as family complaints, arose due to dissatisfaction with the patient's care. Deciding to become a representative demonstrated my desire to serve even more.

Find your gauntlet in life that you can wave in the air for a more significant cause than you. I believe this challenge of making a difference is what it takes to spur you into action and become a champion for that cause. This dogged drive ignites intrinsic motivation, and there is nothing more powerful.

It is about finding opportunities to support your purpose and being open to changes that may come your way to develop your career and provide personal fulfilment. Do you say "NO" more than you say "YES"? Saying yes more is also key to succeeding in life.

Let me tell you another story...

A little boy ran to his father and said, "Dad! Dad! What's the secret to success in life?"

His father replied, ""Son, that is a tough question, and I'm not the one to answer; go ask your mother."

The boy ran to his mother and asked, "Mum! Mum! What's the secret to success in life?"

She replied, "Son, that is a tough question. I'm not the one to answer; ask the Wise One. You will have to wait until summer."

Autumn leaves fell, winter snow covered the ground, and spring flowers bloomed. Summer finally arrived, so the little boy excitedly packed a bag and headed towards the Wise One.

Arriving in the village, he saw many different people from all over waiting to hear the teachings of the Wise One. The little boy waited patiently for his turn.

"Please tell me, what is the secret of success in life?"

"Son, that is a tough question," answered the Wise One. "While I think of an answer, visit my castle and appreciate all its wonder and beauty. Drink everything in, and remember. Take this spoon with you with two drops of oil and be careful not to spill it. Be back in two hours, and I will answer your question."

The little boy returned with the two drops of oil still on the spoon. The Wise One asked him what he had seen and whether he'd appreciated everything.

The boy replied, "No, no, but I still have the two drops of oil."

"My son, go back and appreciate everything you see, hear and feel and return with the two drops of oil on the spoon."

The little boy revisited the castle. He was excited at everything he saw, heard and felt. In his excitement, he dropped the spoon with two drops of oil.

On his return, the Wise One said, "Son, the secret of success in life is very simple. To absorb, understand and use the richness of the world around you, pay attention to every one of your five senses, for each is a priceless gift. Soon you will learn how the whole world conspires to serve you in reaching whatever you want. It would be best to remember to move toward your goals with care and flexibility. As you marvel at the world around, you must equally care about the two drops of oil on your spoon."

Based on a story in The Alchemist by Paulo Coelho

Celebrating success

As I have mentioned previously, it is wise to look for evidence of your opportunity in many nooks and crannies of our world. Remember, success is different for everyone, but there are common traits that each of us must possess. Let's consider the business world for a moment. Large organisations such as Google know the value of celebrating success; that is why each week, they take time out of their business to focus on all the achievements gained that week. They value their workforce, so recognition is part of the recipe for continued success. We all have a basic human need to be recognised, heard and understood.

Learn to celebrate significant achievements such as being awarded a degree as well as those simple steps you take each day. For some, getting out of bed is an achievement; for others, sticking to their plans. Most of us want to find joy and happiness in the simple things in life. You might take time to smell the roses, watch a sunrise or sunset, or spend an evening with your family. Mindfulness is a hot topic in today's world, so you could try it by making an effort; you could make time to listen to the birdsong in the early morning, for example.

The celebration does not need to involve money and it is the free spirit of gratitude that will produce more and more success. So if you want an abundance of success, then learn this simple trait of celebrating every step on your journey

I want to share my top five strategies for celebrating success:

1. Make celebration meaningful. It must be authentic and come from your heart.

2. Recognise your achievements. If you do not recognise them, how can you expect others to do so?

3. Share success stories. People always want to know HOW you did it.

4. Could you pay it forward? When you're celebrating an achievement of your own, show your gratitude by acknowledging the people who helped make it happen. Continually seek opportunities to help other people succeed so that they have a reason to celebrate too.

5. Give a gift of gratitude. Send a handwritten note to those who support and help you achieve your goals.

It's your turn...

Write down five ways in which you celebrate success. Remember to celebrate the small steps as well as the big occasions. Celebrate success every day.

From the beginning of life, whether spurred on by extrinsic motivation from our parents or the developed intrinsic motivation, we are driven to move forward and succeed. One mindset change is to see failure as part of the road to success. Failure allows you to find new solutions, build resilience and strengthen your resourcefulness. Never underestimate its power. There is plenty of evidence in your own life and around you to shift the lens and alter your beliefs to a winning mindset. Following your heart and connecting within are the main driving forces that will enable you to find your purpose. Once you connect with your goal, your confidence rises, and you know that nothing will get in your way of moving the mountains you face each day.

I know you can do anything you put your mind to. How do I know this? Because I did it! Take the first step today. It's your turn. Be the change and make the difference. Your success depends upon it. It's **Time for Purpose**.

Aunty Kate's Learning Points

◊   Define and know what success means for you.

◊   Success looks like a plate of spaghetti – it is not a straight road.

◊   Having a why is crucial, as is setting goals to achieve your vision.

◊   There are many traits and habits needed, such as dedication, commitment and determination to ensure success.

◊   Start with knowing your values.

◊   Look for evidence in your life, in others' lives and metaphors to keep you motivated and focused.

◊   Celebrate all wins, whether small or significant.

One last thing…

Success looks different to different people. Ensure you define and recognise your type of success. It is crucial to measure success, and that takes creating a vision aligned to your values, passion and purpose and setting SMART goals to help you every step of the way. It is vital to your level of resilience, motivation and stamina to perceive failure as part of the road to success. Continue to develop good habits and traits that will ensure you achieve success daily. When needing a boost of confidence and reassurance, look for the evidence within yourself, as well as others and stories. Above all, celebrate every type of success to keep you motivated and focused on becoming the best version of yourself.

Chapter Ten:
Legacy

Strength of Character, Happiness and Fulfilment

The Cambridge Dictionary's definition of legacy is:

Something that is a part of your history, or that remains from an earlier time.

"Legacy is not what's left tomorrow when you're gone. It's what you give, create, impact and contribute today while you're here that then happens to live on."

Rasheed Ogunlaru
British speaker, author, life and business coach

What is a legacy?

When a person dies, the mark an individual leaves on the world represents that individual's legacy. It is about the richness of the individual's life, including what that person accomplished and their impact on people and places. Ultimately, a person's life story reflects the individual's legacy.

What leads to your legacy is deep, and the journey to reveal your purpose that creates the road to a lasting memory is paved with undulations, mountains and oceans to overcome. You should never fear the failures, problems and challenges you face in life, for they are not your weakness, but your most excellent teachers. Changing this limiting mindset will propel you forward in the quest to find your purpose, thus adding meaning, happiness and fulfilment to your life.

Can you answer the question "Who are you?" If not, then how can you leave a legacy? It would help if you understood that life is a journey and that part of your path is to explore who you are and recognise yourself without judgement. The only way to do this is to learn the traits of great leaders who walk their talk and have used their lives to better humankind, thus leaving a lasting memory for their families and the world.

Let me share a story…

The Rev. Desmond Tutu's (1931-2021) life purpose highlighted the unjust, marginalisation and anti-apartheid disparities in his beloved South Africa. He was instrumental in sharing his vision for a better world with America, and Jesse Jackson compared Tutu to the "Martin Luther King of South Africa".

Tutu was also known for his popularisation of the Rainbow Nation as a metaphor for post-apartheid South Africa after 1994, when Nelson Mandela became the first black president of the country. He first used the analogy in 1989 when he described a multiracial protest crowd as the "rainbow people of God". His attention focused on sharing the story that could arguably lead to his greatest legacy of giving an African model for expressing the nature of human community to the world as it entered the twenty-first century.

Tutu was an uncompromising man who focused on his mission of serving God and others with great compassion and the purpose of making the world a more just and peaceful place for all. His work was recognised in the 1984 when he won the Nobel Peace Prize. Tutu's most significant work was to face Truth and Reconciliation as a way to forgive but not forget the past atrocities so that his vision of a more peaceful world could be a new Reality for South Africa.

From Desmond Tutu's story, you can see that he was a man of determination, focus and commitment, three traits necessary for living a life on purpose that leads to happiness and fulfilment. Tutu is the epitome of a man who embodies the term 'strength of character.' Let us now explore what it means to have the strength of character and how you can build yours so you too can become fearless, unstoppable and limitless in your pursuit of being the best version of yourself, to leave a lasting legacy.

Strength of character

According to *Psychology Today* and viacharacter.org, 'strength of character' emphasises six human virtues, and we all possess the 24 strengths of character qualities to varying degrees. This early 2000s research was gathered using scientific methodology, giving it great credibility in today's world.

Like all good science, the researchers devised a classification system that resulted in six virtues based on positive traits of human beings. Their work has gathered momentum, and now you can find many articles online and in scientific publications evidencing the quality and results of their findings in a variety of cultures.

The 24 character strengths organise themselves under the six virtues of: wisdom and knowledge; humanity; justice; courage; temperance; and transcendence.

- **Wisdom and Knowledge** – Strengths of wisdom and knowledge are cognitive strengths related to acquiring and using information. Strengths comprised of this virtue are creativity, curiosity, open-mindedness, love of learning and perspective.

- **Humanity** – Strengths of humanity involve caring interpersonal relationships with others, particularly in one-to-one relationships. Strengths comprised of this virtue are love, kindness and social intelligence.

- **Justice** – Strengths of justice refer to the optimal relationship between the individual and the group or community, rather than the more one-to-one relationships in human virtue. Strengths comprised of this virtue are teamwork, fairness and leadership.

- **Courage** – Strengths of courage involve applying will and fortitude in overcoming internal or external resistance to accomplish goals. Strengths comprised of this virtue are bravery, perseverance, integrity and enthusiasm.

- **Temperance** – Strengths of temperance protect us from excess. Strengths comprised of this virtue are forgiveness, humility, prudence and self-control.

- **Transcendence** – Strengths of transcendence allow people to rise above their troubles and find meaning in the larger universe. The strengths of transcendence are appreciation of beauty and excellence, purpose, gratitude, optimism and humour.

As you can see from the above list, we have already discussed many of these traits throughout the book, aligning with who you want to become, improving outcomes, and living a life of purpose. When you adopt this approach to life, you can leave a legacy through your experiences, learning and teaching.

Strengths of character, such as open-mindedness, kindness, teamwork, integrity, self-control and gratitude, have been illustrated in many stories. You have been encouraged to consider these traits within your life.

It's your turn...

Scan the QR code below to discover your measurement of these 24 character strengths.

Happiness

Happiness is an emotional state considered by feelings of joy, satisfaction, contentment and fulfilment. As we live in a world of duality, to feel happy we have to experience the opposite, which is sadness. The secret is to live life more in the pool of happiness. Do you believe that happiness is a choice? In every situation we experience, we will have to choose how to perceive it, feel it and respond to it.

In 2020, our world erupted into turmoil, uncertainty and restriction due to the global pandemic caused by Covid-19. Many governments legalised 'lockdowns' in numerous countries worldwide, ordering their citizens to stay indoors.

Maslow's Hierarchy of Needs (from the bottom upwards) are: Physiological needs – food and clothing; Safety needs – job security, health; Love and Belonging needs – friendship, family; Esteem – respect, self-esteem, freedom; and Self-actualization – a desire to become the most one can be). These suggest that we were all unnerved. Both our psychological and safety needs were challenged, resulting in people plummeting into a fearful pit associated with a significant health scare, disruption in employment, and personal security. These have all influenced us at a deep subconscious level and will take time, patience and understanding to bounce back from its impact.

Exchanging our happiness for fear and dread took its toll. However, as people became used to the situation, they could add a little happiness into their lives. Once the scientists and medics found a vaccine for Covid-19, people relaxed more and found that they longed for that euphoric sense of joy as restrictions lifted. Feeling happy is essential to our well-being as it releases dopamine, serotonin and endorphins into our bloodstreams that provide that feel-good factor that motivates and inspires us.

From this experience, many people will have re-enforced their resilience, whilst others will take more time to strengthen it once more.

Let me tell you a story...

Experiences of overcoming adversities and challenges in your life strengthen your resilience. I made the conscious choice of making the best out of my new circumstances during the lockdown. I decided Covid-19 was not going to impede my level of happiness. As a woman who loves to be outdoors and busy, I found being able to walk each day a blessing; it improved my mood and gave me the boost I needed to carry on.

I also love sewing, so I was able to find the time that had eluded me before lockdown to reconnect with a particular pastime of making clothes. I was happy when I used my creative skills to make dresses, shorts and skirts for my grandchildren. I even made face masks for my family and friends!

It is vital for your mental health and well-being that you adopt such an open-minded and positive attitude to life. When challenged, you can always find some silver lining that will allow you to choose happiness over sadness, anxiety and stress.

I have intimated that happiness is a choice, so how can you ensure that you choose to be happy? You know the analogy that you need to put on your oxygen mask first before helping others? Then your happiness needs to be before others. This behaviour and thinking is something many women find incredibly challenging. When women become mothers, an instinct seems to take over, and they put everyone else's needs and happiness before their own.

One way to overcome this limiting perspective is to find the courage to go on an inner journey. As children, we are on that inner path, but it is quickly overtaken by the external messages and learning we receive from our parents, culture and community. Only once the pressures of life become too much do we reach a pivotal point where enough is enough and decide to take a different path. After all, as Einstein once said, "Insanity is doing the same thing over and over and expecting different results."

Once you choose this new path, you get different and exciting results. One of the most significant results is learning that choosing happiness is up to you. Like all habits, it embeds itself over time, so you need to practice it daily with a conscious mind. So the next time you find yourself thinking negatively, ask yourself, "How can I change this feeling and choose a better one that has happiness attached to it?"

Another way to be happier is to make time to do the things that bring you joy. Perhaps you like playing a musical instrument, drawing or doing craftwork? You may love doing physical activities outdoors, such as walking in nature, running or sightseeing. You must take the time to do what YOU love. Join groups with like-minded people and make time to spend with family and friends. It's all about balance and harmony in life, leading to greater happiness.

Travelling broadens the mind and feeds your soul. Learning about new places, cultures and people is uplifting and offers opportunities to do things you may not have even considered in the past. Tasting fresh foods, learning new languages and participating in cultural practices all feed your inner happiness. You can use these beautiful experiences to shift your mood if you slip back into darker places. Remind yourself of these fun times, look at photographs and talk about them to your family and friends. These conversations spark happiness that you can revisit when you feel down. Happiness is the driving force that allows you to try new things and enjoy your life.

Quite often, people say they are feeling sad or down, and when you suggest that they choose a different emotion, such as happiness, they tell you that they 'can't'. The word 'can't' continues to feed the negativity. It needs reframing with the positive comment, 'I can'. Instead, think of a happy time or choose to do something you love, then you automatically change your thought pattern and begin to feel uplifted. Remember, happiness is a choice. I have said it once, and I'll say it again. Once you start practising this new habit, your mood lifts, and you can tap into a better spirit anytime you choose.

"Tap into your happiness by doing what you love."
Aunty Kate

Fulfilment

Fulfilment is a higher-order thinking concept so understanding its meaning is crucial to achieving its significance to the fullest.

The dictionary definition of fulfilment is:

> The achievement of something desired, promised, or predicted.

To be fulfilled, you attach it to emotions. Fulfilment is a happy, contented feeling. Some people achieve fulfilment from being a parent, having a great job, or graduating from school. People often feel it with the completion of something, whether it's a goal, dream, or vision. Feeling fulfilled usually makes you think of something longer-term than a quick fix when you think about feeling fulfilled. In some ways, you could argue that this is true; however, I believe that you can attach a sense of fulfilment to small bite-size steps towards your bigger goals and visions. Everything in life depends on your experiences and how you use these to influence your perception of many things. You can have one situation with two people looking at it, offering two very different outcomes

Let me tell you a story...

Two mums tell their children that they will be going on a picnic the next day. They are all excited about going on a picnic with their respective families. The children go off to bed, and the mums prepare the picnic basket for the next day.

The children excitedly get up and look out the window in the morning. Instead of the sunshine they were expecting, it is raining cats and dogs. The children's faces slump as they know that their plans will not come to fruition.

The first mum turns to her children and says, "Never mind. We can go on the picnic tomorrow when the sun is expected to shine." The children look sad and go back to their rooms.

The second mum turns to her children and says, "Never mind. We can take our picnic and go down into the basement, spread the blanket on the floor, and still enjoy our picnic." The children jump for joy and dash straight down to the basement.

This story illustrates how two people can think differently about the same situation. Different circumstances present how you decide to perceive them. Some people carry the sunny weather inside of them constantly and look for the silver lining and alternative opportunities in adverse situations. One mum allowed the inclement weather to interfere with her plans. In contrast, the other mum had a more optimistic outlook and found a way to ensure her children did not experience disappointment. What would you do in the same situation?

Let's explore further some of the things people need to do (take action) to find fulfilment in their lives, instead of finding excuses as to why they cannot achieve it. We have already discovered that your perception and mindset significantly influence your decisions.

Next, I would ask you to consider cultural narratives which often send us messages that we are not enough and that true happiness comes from external objects. The issue with this message is that, no matter how much wealth we acquire, there is always something better. Things start to lose their appeal soon after your acquisition, and you always want more. The truth is that real happiness doesn't come from the exterior.

Fulfilment comes from witnessing your growth. When you're able to hit the pause button and reflect on the substantial changes in your life, you feel a sense of meaning and purpose. Practising gratitude for these changes propels you with the motivation to continue striving for success and makes all of your sacrifices worthwhile.

When you learn this powerful life skill, you can use it to shape your philosophy and share it with others so that you can leave a lasting legacy.

Aunty Kate's Learning Points

◊ A purpose is your birthright, and partly to leave your legacy like a footprint in the sand of time.

◊ Legacy is the richness of the tapestry you leave behind.

◊ Become aware of your character strengths and continuously develop them.

◊ There are the six virtues of wisdom and knowledge; humanity; justice; courage; temperance; and transcendence.

◊ Know that happiness is an inside job; choose it always and nurture it wisely

◊ Tap into your happiness by doing what you love.

◊ Find your purpose, and you will achieve the elusive sense of fulfilment that all humans desire. You will know it when you live a life of happiness, love and peace.

One last thing...

We all want to leave a legacy, but it takes much exploration, discovery and commitment. It's about having awakened awareness, a life of service, and leaving a mark on the world through your creativity, dedication and commitment. Build your character strengths to keep you focused, wise and virtuous. Remember, you have the power to do anything and be anyone you intend. Know that happiness is an inside job, and the most extraordinary journey you can have in life is the inner journey to your passion and purpose to leave your legacy.

Kate and her four children

Further Reading and References

Books

Coelho, Paulo, *The Alchemist*, HarperCollins (2012)

Dweck, Dr Carol, *Mindset: A New Psychology of Success*, Ballantine Books (2007)

Enoto, Dr Masaru, *The Hidden Messages in Water*, Pocket Books (2005)

Frankl, Viktor, *Man's Search for Meaning*, Rider (2004)

Lindenfield, Gael, *Assert Yourself: Simple Steps to Build Your Confidence*, HarperNonFiction (2014)

Owen, Nick, *The Magic of Metaphor: 77 Stories for Teachers, Trainers & Thinkers*, Crown House Publishing (2000)

Scott, Sir Walter, *Tales of a Grandfather, Vol I*, Forgotten Books (2018)

Sinek, Simon, *Start With Why: How Great Leaders Inspire Everyone to Take Action*, Penguin (2011)

Magazines

Psychology Today

Journals

Fletcher, D and Sarkar, M, (2013) Psychological resilience: A review and critique of definitions, concepts, and theory. *European Psychologist*, 18(1), 12–23

Online Articles

www.successstory.com/inspiration/why-success-is-important-to-us

www.healthline.com/health/fitness-exercise/how-to-increase-stamina

www.thewellnessenterprise.com/emoto/

www.mindsetopia.com/why-success-is-important/

www.ecowatch.com/8-shocking-facts-about-water-consumption-1881989567.html

www.positivepsychology.com/resilience-theory/

www.jennynurick.com/how-to-be-assertive/

www.verywellmind.com/glossophobia-2671860

www.online.maryville.edu/blog/self-empowerment/

www.psychologytoday.com/gb/blog/how-do-life/201705/developing-drive

Other Websites

www.viacharacter.org

www.betterhealth.com

www.volunteeringjourneys.com

www.ncvo.org.uk

Margie Meacham: www.learningtogo.info

Daniel Pink: www.danpink.com

Dylan Buckley: www.dbuckley.contently.com

Acknowledgements

I would like to thank my mentor and book coach, Brenda Dempsey, who spent hours upon hours making my dreams come true. Her professionalism, patience and foresight turned the person I am and my career into reality. Her exceptional guidance is remarkable and very much appreciated.

The very first time we met on Zoom, we talked briefly about writing a book; she championed it and helped me to arrive at many ideas that are reflected in this book. I am so fortunate that I came across Brenda, when I merely thought about writing my second book.

Publishing a book requires a team effort, as well as talented experts who are supportive and experienced. A special thank you to the team – Zara Thatcher and Olivia Eisinger – for the excellent work they did. The phone calls, emails, WhatsApp messages, spending hours editing the draft, and supporting me in proofreading my manuscript to help get the best out of my story. You turned the manuscript into a book. I am indebted to you.

I want to express my profound gratitude to H.E. Dr. O. Favour Ayodele, who despite his jam-packed busy schedule, accepted the invitation to write the Foreword for this book. I am grateful to have you, Dr Favour; you responded so promptly to my request, I am very lucky to earn your attention.

Special thanks to Yetunde Adeshile, who has been very supportive and always ready to lend a helping hand. You worked so hard with me in preparing my conferences, especially the art work; I am very grateful.

A special thank you to Felicity Okolo who helped me to write my autobiography.

To all the groups and organisation that I belong to, I want to say thank you for giving me the opportunity to be a member.

My siblings – Ichie Arinze (*Nwachinemelu*), Barrister Edozie (*Ikeoha*), Chief Amechi Ezeasor (*Akulueuno Nanka*), Mr. Chukwudi, Mr. Polycarp and my one and only sister, Louinne. Growing up together was challenging, especially the period of the civil war, but we shared those challenges with love, joy and fun.

You all made me who I am today as your big sister. You are always there to protect me; I value your unconditional support and understanding. Thank you.

I thank my late father, Chief Fidelis Ezeobuoha Ezeasor (*Okwuolisa*), whose belief in gender equality gave me the opportunity to excel in education and follow my dreams, despite his friends telling him it was a waste of money to invest in a girl child. My life cannot be what it is today without this single act. "The Papa" as I always call him, Daalu (*thank you*) and I miss you two dearly.

My late mother, "Mama Ayi"(*our mother*), as we always called her, Princess Veronica Egbeichi Ezeasor (*Okwesilieze Umuagbala*), you taught me so much about good qualities of life such as humility, leadership skills, strength, stamina and how to gain respect in the community. I have been able to emulate some of these qualities, and that has helped me to cope with so many types of people that I have come across, especially women. "Mama Ayi, anam ekene gi. Daalu, Na nudo."(*Our mother, I am greeting you, thank you, go in peace.*)

Thank you to my late husband, Ifeanyichukwu Festus Anolue, who kept the promise he made to my father, by allowing me to continue with my education. You supported me throughout my nurse and midwifery training. You were my husband, father, soulmate and friend. You are just one in a million. Rest in perfect peace.

My GT sisters – Chioma Obi-Nwagwu, Christine Adamu and Maggi Chukwudi. Going on cruise with you three was great fun and an unforgettable experience. You've all become a special part of my life and I cherish you all. Going to theatre, spa, parties, cinema, dinner and networking, wahoooo! I am really having much fun post-retirement.

My appreciation also go to the traditional ruler of Nanka, HRH Godwin Ezekuniye Ezeilo Ezeadusionu (*Obu Nanka*), his Cabinet and Chiefs, including Onowu Kofi Obijiofor (*Ajie Nanka*), Chief Dr. Poly Emenike (*Odenigbo Nanka*), Chief Ebere Nwosu (*Ezeudo Nanka*), Chief Damian Okeke (*Ogene Nanka*)

I like to give a huge thanks to all the wonderful people for sparing a moment out of their busy schedule to read my book and write testimonials. I know how busy you can be and I thank you all immensely. I am ever so grateful that you were able to support me by creating time to endorse the book. I value those hours you spent reading the manuscript; my heartfelt gratitude to you all – you made my expectation a reality. I am very lucky.

Finally, I would like to give a big thanks to all of you and those who passed through my life, whom I may fail to mention. You are numerous in number, but you are a significant part of my journey.

About the Author

D r Kate Anolue was born in Jos, Plateau State, Nigeria. After the devastating civil war in Nigeria, she moved to the UK to be with her husband. She became a midwife but tragedy struck when she became a widow with four young children, including a baby of 18 months.

Kate picked herself up and worked hard as a midwife, helping other women in difficult situations. She went on to study law and became an expert in medical negligence cases in birth and midwifery care, advising both new mothers and the maternity unit. She has given 40 years' service to the NHS.

Kate is a woman of action, duty and purpose. She is presently a serving councillor in her Borough of Enfield in north London and has been so for over 20 years. And her ultimate service to the Borough of Enfield was becoming the Mayor – not once, but twice! In 2016, Kate launched 'Catch Them Young' to inspire the young into politics and leadership. Through this initiative, she was able to introduce the

Young Mayor and Deputy Young Mayor to Enfield during her second mayoral tenure. She was given the Freedom of the Borough of Enfield for her tireless service to the community and was recognised in September 2019 as a 'Greater Londoner' by BBC London, as someone who does great things for the community.

Kate never rests on her laurels! She is currently the CEO of Tender Care Health Initiative, providing a one-stop-shop for vulnerable and young mothers. In addition, she is the Founder and President of Forum for Africans, African Caribbean and Asian Women in Politics.